PREPARING EDUCATIONAL MATERIALS

NEW PATTERNS OF LEARNING SERIES

Edited by P.J. Hills, University of Surrey

AN INTRODUCTION TO EDUCATIONAL COMPUTING
Nicholas John Rushby

PREPARING EDUCATIONAL MATERIALS
N.D.C. Harris

THE ORGANISATION AND MANAGEMENT OF
EDUCATIONAL TECHNOLOGY
Richard N. Tucker

PREPARING EDUCATIONAL MATERIALS

N.D.C. HARRIS

CROOM HELM LONDON

© 1979 N.D.C. Harris
Croom Helm Ltd. 2-10, St John's Road, London SW11

British Library Cataloguing in Publication Data
Harris, Norman Duncan Campany
    Preparing educational materials
    (New patterns of learning series).
    1. Teaching — Aids and devices
    I. Title II. Series
    371.3'078   LB1043

ISBN 0-85664-932-5

Printed in Great Britain by offset lithography by
Billing & Sons Ltd, Guildford, London and Worcester

CONTENTS

NEW PATTERNS OF LEARNING

The Purpose of This Series

This series of books is intended to provide readable introductions to trends and areas of current thinking in education. Each book will be of interest to all educators, trainers and adminstrators responsible for the implementation of educational policies and programmes in higher, further and continuing education.

The books are designed for easy access of information. Each contains a glossary of important terms in the subject and has an annotated bibliography of key works to enable the reader to pursue selected areas in depth should he or she so wish.

This, the second book in the series, *Preparing Educational Materials*, is written by Duncan Harris of the University of Bath where he is Director of the Science and Technology Education Centre.

The first title in this series is *An Introduction to Educational Computing* by Nicholas Rushby of the Imperial College Computer Centre, London.

P.J. Hills
Guildford, 1979

ACKNOWLEDGEMENTS

I wish to thank many people who contributed ideas and criticisms to the book. My research students and students doing a full time masters' course at the University of Bath generated many of the ideas or criticised mine. In particular I would wish to mention Peter Smith, Javad Tafreshi Hashemi, Professor W.H. Dowdeswell at the University of Bath and Professor H. Good of Queens University, Kingston, Ontario. Professor Good and my father-in-law, Mr Wilfred Georgeson offered criticism and encouragement when I had completed the first draft. Dr Phil Hills, the editor of the series, gave me detailed critical and constructive comments from which the book has developed even further.

I wish to thank Mrs Gill Colston for her patience in dealing with the vagaries of my writing and for typing and re-typing the final draft.

Finally I wish to thank my wife and daughters for their encouragement and patience when I was seldom available to help with the house, the garden, homework or revision!

N.D.C. Harris

Dedicated to my wife

INTRODUCTION

Traditional methods of teaching in continuing, further and higher education are the lecture, the tutorial and practical work. Variations have developed which include seminars, problems classes, project work and the use of a range of audio visual materials and materials designed to enable students to learn by themselves. Formerly the dominant tradition in the United Kingdom was that of the lecturer as teacher; now recent developments are showing a common basis in the assumption that the student is the learner.

Whatever models are used for designing courses and curricula, a wide range of educational materials is now available. These vary from the use of the chalkboard, books, hand-outs and audio visual materials, to tests, examinations, assignments and projects. Obviously these materials vary from those produced by a lecturer or on the lecturer's initiative, to those which the student produces largely on his own initiative.

In writing a short book of this kind the author has to bear in mind several assumptions about those who might read it. A reader could have little or no experience or theoretical background, or he might be an expert with a range of theoretical knowledge and experience. It is hoped that a critical appraisal of this book will lead to constructive development of a reader's role as adviser on or as preparer of educational materials.

Readers will also vary in their approach. The book has not been assembled with the assumption that the reader will start at the beginning and read through to the end. Some readers may find Chapters 9-12 the best starting point. These chapters are on the management of learning and are written in a prescriptive style with the assumption that the reader pursues further those areas that interest him

Chapters 2-8 adopt a different style; not only are questions posed to which there may be no clear-cut answers, but also quite dogmatic statements are made which it is intended that the reader should query. In early chapters some diagrams have been given which show the contents of the chapter. Some readers may find these a useful means of summarising the content or developing their own diagrams.

At the end of the book is a glossary of terms giving brief explanations of the range of terms used. There is an annotated bibliography, which although in no way intended to be complete, gives some indication of the sources of the author's ideas and which can be used to read further into the subject.

1 EDUCATIONAL MATERIALS

How Can Courses Be Improved?

One reason for a reader's interest in this book may be a desire to improve the courses that he organises. It is often reasoned, quite falsely, that through change and innovation come better learning experiences for students. However it must be borne in mind that the bigger the change the less likely it is that the effects can be predicted. One should also beware of initiating change for the sake of it, particularly in content or by the addition of new content brought about by the development of knowledge within the discipline. The question should be considered whether new developments ought to be incorporated and what effect this would have on student learning or problem-solving techniques.

Another reason for change is to overcome problems which have occurred in a particular facet of a course. These problems may be administrative (e.g. more students and the same amount of space), tutorial (e.g. the loss of a member of staff who has not been replaced), or learning problems (e.g. regular poor performance by students on certain parts of the course).

These kinds of changes can be referred to as 'patching' and 'hole plugging' exercises. From an educational point of view there is no basic change to the course as a whole. Often the patching exercise is carried out without consideration of evidence from other institutions or of a clear investigation of the possible effects of the change.

Any change, large or small, is heavily constrained by available resources. In order to overcome these constraints, considerable time and effort have been spent in developing new courses based on changes of teaching methods. Usually such exercises are carefully planned and checked for further modification. Perhaps the checks and continual hole plugging are typical of higher and further education where courses are always under development and never in their final state. The Open University, for example, uses a course design system which after a careful initial design appears to carry out hole plugging and patching in a formal, systematic way.

Unfortunately, in some institutions many changes, developments and innovations are carried out without any consultation with the

11

learners (past or present). In a world where cost effectiveness is becoming more and more the norm, the omission of students from planning exercises may be unfortunate both pragmatically and politically. I am not suggesting that students know best (particularly on content and method), but they do have more recent experience on the learning side of the fence than the lecturers. In my experience students are not only co-operative, but also remarkably astute in pin-pointing problems; their solution to problems may at times be conservative, but they will respond to radical solutions and show enthusiasm whilst pointing out likely problems.

Adopting a Systematic Approach

Adopting a systematic approach is one means by which recent research and experimental evidence can be incorporated into existing schemes. Whereas earlier work was heavily dependent on the use of objectives and test procedures, more recent work is based for the most part on the process of learning and in particular the styles of learning used by students.

In this book there is a general theme related to these more recent approaches. The perspective of knowledge is seen from the provision of packages to the solving of problems, and the learner's personal exploration of the situation. The materials provided for the learner are either highly structured, loosely structured or unstructured. However, whichever is used, it is possible to be systematic in the organisation and evaluation of the learning environment. Possibly the keyword is management. In this book management has been subdivided into four areas using a musical analogy: the performer, the conductor, the composer and the critic.

The management is based on various factors — communication, the process of learning, the levels of learning, the assessment of learning, and the modes and media of learning. Each factor involves the lecturer and the student and it is possible to approach from the factors to the management (the order of the chapters in the book), or from the management to the factors (when Chapters 9-12 would be read first).

The Roles of Performer, Conductor, Composer, Critic

The musical analogy helps to highlight the roles of the lecturer in his job. In many learning situations the lecturer is required to assume the role of the performer whether as a soloist in a lecture, one of a team in a course, an accompaniment role to support and encourage the students, or as the leader of a group of students in a seminar. A performer needs a professional approach based on experience and theoretical expertise associated with technique and practice.

The conductor assembles all the orchestra and endeavours to produce his interpretation of the score to the best of the orchestra's ability. Some conductors are aggressive, some persuasive and others interactive with the orchestra. In the same way each lecturer varies in his approach towards students.

In musical terms the performance depends on the score and its careful preparation. In a similar way the students' learning is dependent on the ground being prepared for their expected role and for that role to be made clear.

Finally few performances take place without criticism by the performers, the conductor, the composer and the professional critic. Similarly in a learning environment, through the collective views of the learners, the performers, the conductor, the composer and the external critic, improved learning can take place.

The remaining chapters will endeavour to clarify the needs of the lecturer's role and of the learners' role. All aspects depend however on there being adequate communication channels between the lecturer and the learners.

2 THE NATURE OF COMMUNICATION

Human Communications

In today's world a wide variety of media of communication are playing an ever increasing part (McLuham, 1964). The use of computers associated with television displays on an international network have enormous potential in the field of education.

Whenever people communicate with each other many problems are bound to arise. Take this book as an example. Not only do I have problems in expressing my thoughts and ideas in words but also the interaction between you and me can pose problems. From what you read you develop some picture of me, I have a different picture of myself, and then there is me as I really am — and the same applies to you! So immediately we have a $3 \times 3 (= 9)$ way possible interaction. When this is multiplied for a group of thirty, a hundred, or two hundred students who are attending a lecture . . . The best one can manage is a compromise. The compromise can be considered as an overlap between ideas. One's aim is to ensure that the overlap is as great as possible. Complete overlap, i.e. perfect communication, is obviously impossible, but the situation where there is no overlap must be avoided. Let us look at one or two elements in this communication process.

It is clear that students and lecturers have different past experiences. The lecturer will have experience of the discipline in which he is communicating. More overlap is likely to occur between ideas if the lecturer uses vocabulary and conceptual frameworks which are familiar to the student. If he uses only his own framework he is more likely to produce no communication — hardly a good basis for learning.

The ability of the human memory to discriminate and to retain information is limited. Experimental evidence suggests that our senses and memory tend to be limited to about seven bits of information (Miller, 1970), so for the purposes of retaining information and ideas we often use up to about seven headings or key words.

Other learners find mnemonics a useful aid to memory, whilst yet others associate ideas with well-known visual features. If one is to communicate successfully with students there is a need to help them to produce their own framework of learning, rather than to impose our

14

own, for whereas key words help some, mnemonics or visual features may help others.

Some Barriers to Communication

Parry (1967) lists seven basic barriers as follows:

1. Limitation of the receiver's capacity.
2. Distraction (noise).
3. The unstated assumption.
4. Incompatibility of schemas.
5. Intrusion of unconscious or partly conscious mechanisms.
6. Confused presentation.
7. Absence of communication facilities.

Let us consider each of these in turn.

Limitation of Receiver's Capacity

Here this is seen in terms of short-term and long-term memory. The short-term memory is thought to last for a few seconds and long-term memory over a much longer period of time. In order to extend the memory span the mind develops patterns of ideas, but if ideas are presented in such a way that the pattern developed is confusing, then the information is rejected because it is beyond the receiver's capacity.

Distraction (Noise)

The phenomenon of distraction is familiar to us in many contexts. At a party we may find ourselves listening to another conversation rather than the one in which we are involved (technically 'noise'). The atmosphere in a room, heat, noise, uncomfortable seating, etc., all contribute to distraction. Other sources of distraction can be tooth-ache, headache — again competing stimuli or noise. An important form of distraction is unfamiliar language — or an excess of jargon which, if it is unfamiliar to the learner, constitutes noise.

The Unstated Assumption

This speaks for itself. A barrier to communication can be built up because the communicator makes assumptions about the receiver's basic knowledge.

Incompatability of Schemas

One problem in communication lies in the interpretation of the information received. For communication to occur interpretation is essential, but if the experience and background of the receiver are very different from that of the transmitter (for example a foreign student with a very different cultural background attending a course based on Western culture), the interpretation can be very different from that intended. We can say that there is an incompatibility of schemas. The schema can be interpreted as the enduring patterns of brain activity based on experience. This is a very important area of communication. The overlap of schemas between the lecturer and the learner is crucial to learning, for the schemas do not only relate to knowledge but also to feelings and reactions.

Intrusion of Unconscious or Partly Conscious Mechanisms

The unconscious or partly conscious mechanisms include worry, fear, love, hidden persuasion, etc., all of which can inhibit or prevent communication. If the communication is prevented, learning is obviously affected.

Confused Presentation

It is in this area that care is needed in the selection of print format, in the acceptable norms of audio visual production and even in the performance of the lecturer and his chalkboard presentation.

Absence of Communication Facilities

The impersonal relationship between large organisations (whether the Civil Service, large multinational industrial concerns or large trades unions) and the individual often produces an alienation of the individual. The resulting unwillingness even to try to develop and maintain a relationship leads to absence of communication channels.

Again, the lecturer who is still talking at 11.59 a.m. in a lecture supposed to end at 12.00 noon is guilty of blocking communication channels. It is a one-way communication, not a reciprocal communication. With no response there is no information and no interpretation.

The lecturer can be considered to be an intermediary between the discipline and the learner. He may be the vital communication link. Without his interpretation, in the lecture room or through independent learning materials, the learner's task is much more difficult. We all tend to hide our uncertainties behind a wall of jargon and a disciplinary superstructure, which are guaranteed to produce immediate barriers. The learner will probably do better if we admit our deficiencies and endeavour to solve the problems together.

One further barrier is perhaps unique to the generation of students now in higher and further education. Not only are there the usual problems of incompatibility of schemas because of changes in society, but also students who now enter further and higher education have spent a larger proportion of their time watching television. There does seem to be some truth in McLuhan's belief (1964) that the students' thought patterns may be very different from those of their elders because of this. Yet education continues to be heavily print-oriented in presentation and in the assessment of a learner's performance.

Communication and the Student

The lecturer's communication problem is partly associated with the variations in student learning patterns. A variety of classifications of learning patterns exists. Some simplified versions are discussed briefly here. The two lists below have some common thread, although ther terms are certainly not synonymous.

1. Sequential (serialist or atomist)   Holist
2. Repetitive   Creative
3. Converger   Diverger
4. All 'learning' done by external agency   Own learning
5. Haptic   Visual

Taking each pair separately, let us consider the learning patterns. The overlaps between categories will become clear as the lists are considered.

Sequential (Serialist or Atomist)   v. Holist

From evidence in the United Kingdom (Pask, 1975) and from Sweden (Marton, 1975) it seem that students can be divided into those who are dependent on linear relationships (e.g. lists) and a substructure of learning (sequential, serialist, atomist), and those who see a whole picture which they elaborate themselves (holist). From a lecturer's point of view this division presents a problem, because students with extremes of either trait appear to find it difficult to learn from material presented in the other form. Students who are mid-way between the styles may well be able to change from one style to another.

Repetitive v. Creative

Students who learn best in sequential form also tend to present written assignments in a similar form to that presented to them (repetitive). This type of student may perform well in standard examinations which expect a large degree of repetition of factual or analytical material. The students who learn in holist style will certainly not return information as presented, because their learning pattern depends on an overview and not a sequential approach.

Converger v. Diverger

The repetitive student (converger) is more likely to produce what he thinks the lecturer expects, wheras those who are holists tend to diverge. Consequently in examinations in some disciplines the former group will be penalised, in other disciplines the latter group will be penalised.

All 'Learning' Done by an External Agency v. Own Learning

Convergent learners tend to expect the organisation of the learning to be done for them. The converger's learning is usually based on lectures and texts and he expects the 'learning' to be done for him by that method. The diverger on the other hand devises his own methods and is as a result less dependent. However, his learning may not be recognised by the lecturer because it does not always conform to conventional patterns.

Haptic v. Visual

Superimposed on these variations is a similar pattern of visual learning and creativity. The same symptoms of atomistic (haptic) and holist (visual) are present. Each characteristic has its strengths and weaknesses.

Recent work by Entwistle and his colleagues at the University of Lancaster (Entwistle and Percy, 1974) suggest that for a student to be successful in the present system of further and higher education he must be: well-qualified on entry; highly motivated; able; and introverted. He must also be able to work long hours and should have good study methods.

All of these factors must be taken into account as possible variables in the design of instructional materials as will be seen from the following account.

Can Educational Materials Match All Student Types?

One solution is to provide alternative strategies or to provide learning materials which allow each student to develop according to his needs. A weakness here is that if there is to be any comparative assessment, it is difficult to make comparisons on different bases for each student.

Using the simple grouping of students considered in the previous section, what sort of learning materials might match the learning styles? Let us take some fairly obvious examples from which one can begin to judge the possibilities of other formats. To be quite certain about a match between format and student type it is necessary to carry out some experimental work with students.

For a sequential learner, a sequential style of putting elements together could be suitable. The linear sequence of headings shown below would be useful for a learner with this style of learning, but it would be difficult for a holist.

For a holist, a pattern more like that shown in the patterned note on page 21 would be helpful. Obviously the pattern will *not* be the same as mine. You might care to draw your own patterned notes of this chapter and compare them with mine. A sequential learner may find some help from the patterned note, but this seems unlikely.

The convergent sequential learner will probably find programmed learning materials useful for learning. Such materials may be of no use at all to a holist, especially if the programmed material is designed in small steps (frames). The divergent holist learner will find unstructured materials better. The question then inevitably arises as to whether assessment procedures are biased towards one kind of learner, or indeed whether the learning facilities provided are biased towards one kind of learner.

A Linear Sequence of Note Headings on This Chapter

The Nature of Communication

1. Human Communication
   (a) varieties
   (b) overlap of ideas
   (c) variation in experience
   (d) memory

2. Barriers to Communication
   (a) limitation of receiver's capacity
   (b) distraction

(c) unstated assumption
(d) incompatibility of schemas
(e) intrusion of unconscious or partly conscious mechanism
(f) confused presentation
(g) absence of communication facilities

3. Communication and the Student
    (a) learning patterns
        (i) sequential *v.* holist
        (ii) repetitive *v.* creative
        (iii) converger *v.* diverger
        (iv) all learning provided *v.* own learning
        (v) haptic *v.* visual
    (b) 'successful' student and assessment

4. Can Educational Materials Match All Student Types?
    (a) feasibility of compromise
    (b) linear notes and sequential repetitive convergers
    (c) patterned notes — all things to all men?
    (d) does visual style affect pattern?

5. Communication and the Lecturer
    (a) lecturer styles — authoritarian, democratic, organised, disorganised
    (b) knowledge level
    (c) performance

6. Group Communication

Communication and the Lecturer

In the same way that there are different learning styles for learners, there are different teaching styles for lecturers. In a learning environment a compromise is inevitable between the needs of the learner and those of the lecturer. If the lecturer is aware of his style, he may be able to assist learners who use other styles by showing them possible ways of coping with his methods.

One of the biggest difficulties for a lecturer is to utilise efficiently his own pattern of behaviour, particularly if he is at the extremes of being an organised or disorganised person. The systematically organised lecturer probably has a series of headings for his presentation, supporting materials to fit in at the appropriate time, with overhead projector transparencies, 35 mm slides and hand outs pre-prepared.

A Patterned Note

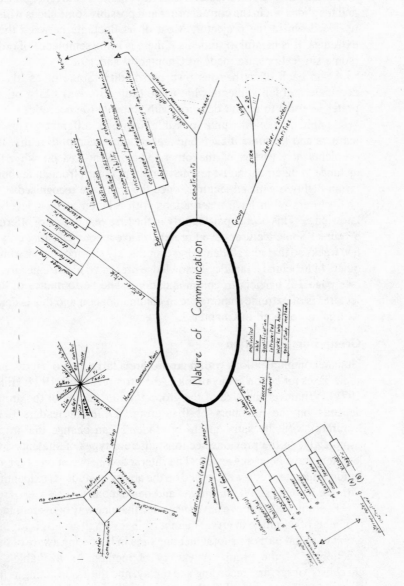

The wholly disorganised lecturer may have his notes barely organised, and his slides not in the correct order and possibly some slides will be upside down in the projector. Most of us fluctuate between these extremes. It is helpful to students if there is some semblance of order (some suggestions are made in Chapters 9 and 10).

Again each of us has his own personality. Some of us like to dominate and tell students what to do (authoritarian) whilst others prefer to come to a joint decision with students (democratic).

Communication is quite possible between different styles of learners and lecturers if each one makes some attempt to realise the problems and wishes of the other. There is no reason why, for instance, a divergent holist learner should not learn from an authoritarian highly organised lecturer, once the traits are recognised.

Lecturers often have reservations with relation to their level of knowledge. This occurs particularly in the first year or two of offering a course. Some lecturers even prefer to have a course lasting only a few weeks so that 'the students don't rumble my shortcomings', whilst others hide behind a façade of knowledge presented in extreme jargon (see page 15, barriers to communication). The performance of the lecturer is of extreme importance in communication and this is dealt with in more detail in Chapter 9.

Group Communication

Human communications within groups are a large area of study, but some bases for action are available (Abercrombie, 1960, 1974; Hills, 1979). Whatever the size of the group the functioning of the group depends on the members of that group. Different leaders (e.g. lecturers) with the same group of students can change the group completely. In the previous sections different types of students and lecturers have been suggested. The interaction between one type of lecturer and the group will depend on the ability of students to identify with the lecturer's style, attitudes and demeanour.

The studies cited above have suggested that one way of overcoming problems of variation in group membership for small groups is for the group to spend part of its total meeting time in becoming aware of the functioning of the group. A variety of methods is available — checklists, observers, recording and replay, and the group acting as its own evaluation system. The time spent in understanding the way in which the group functions appears to produce a considerably improved performance in terms of learning and provides more satisfaction for the participants.

3 PROCESSES OF LEARNING

Taking Notes from Lectures, Books and Journals

Much of the process of learning is in the student's hands. The lecturer can act as an intermediary, a motivator, and can assist with problems. However in continuing or higher education many students arrive with a very limited knowledge on writing notes, organising their study and their time.

There are no hard and fast rules for taking notes during lectures. However there are possibilities which can at least be shown to students. When presenting a lecture or guiding students in their note-taking it could be helpful to limit the number of headings to not more than seven and similar numbers of sub-headings (this was discussed in Chapter 2). It may help students if they are advised to use a similar heading/sub-heading system with some use of colour for emphasis — this type of note is called a linear note, for example:

PROCESSES OF LEARNING
Taking Notes
from (a) lectures;
     (b) books;
     (c) journals.

Some students find it useful to write on alternate pages, using the facing page for further notes derived from reading around the subject. As a general rule gaps, spaces, or blank pages within notes are an aid to visualising notes.

The linear note format is not easy for students who use a more holistic view of subjects; for them a patterned format, as shown on page 22, is probably more acceptable. In this format not only are the elements shown but interrelationships can also be shown.

The advantage of the patterned format for learning purposes would seem to be that:

(1) the pattern is idiosyncratic, enabling the learner to relate to his own experience;
(2) the pattern is analytical and to some extent creative, enabling the learner to take a more active part in the learning.

The patterned note has almost the potential to act as evidence of learning in its own right. From the pattern drawn by the student, the lecturer can deduce the elements and relationships which a student deems to be important, and these can form a useful basis for discussion. In contrast the linear note format is basically a use of someone else's arrangement.

In this chapter various learning processes will be illustrated and ways of practising with students are suggested to help them in the learning process.

In a lecture situation it is worth using part of an early lecture to let students take their own notes, perhaps with no guidance. A suggested routine is shown below. The actual act of stopping and reading the notes after twenty to thirty minutes will have the added advantages of (a) improvement in retention (Bligh, 1972); (b) providing information on what other students think is important. The discussion with other students on what is considered important may encourage a more flexible approach from the learner.

Suggested Routine for Helping Students to Write Lecture Notes

This uses the approach developed by Northedge and Gibbs (see Gibbs, 1976).

1. Allow students to take their own notes for 20-30 minutes.
2. Ask pairs of students to compare notes for differences for about 5 minutes.
3. Ask groups of four students to come to a consensus view for about 10 minutes.
4. Allow groups to report back. (You may be tempted to add your ideas — but let the students have their opportunity first.)

A further suggestion regarding the use of syndicates can be made to students early in their study career. A syndicate is a group of learners who meet regularly (say, three half-hours each week) and question one another on work carried out over the two or three previous days; this will again aid retention and encourage flexibility. It is important that such groups are (a) rigorous in the use of the time and (b) have students who are compatible with one another (Rowntree, 1977; Bligh, 1976).

How do students learn to write notes from materials in printed form? The following routine can form a useful basis for practice, and it is worth spending at least one hour on practising this with students.

Routine for Practising Note-Taking from a Short Paper (Gibbs, 1976)

1. Provide students with a short paper (4/5 sides A4, for example).
2. Ask students to start reading, saying that you will give them time to read all the paper.
3. After about three minutes, stop them reading. Ask them to write down what the paper is about.
4. After another few minutes ask them to compare with their neighbour.
5. After a further few minutes ask groups of four to look for common elements.
6. Now allow time for all to read the paper.
7. Give them 2-3 minutes to write down what the paper is about.
8. Ask pairs to spend 5 minutes looking for differences in their summary.
9. Ask groups of four to spend 10 minutes coming to a consensus view.
10. If there is time, allow groups time to report (a) on consensus; (b) on where most of consensus view actually occurs in the paper.

The paper should be selected because (a) it has a good overview both in the introduction (say two paragraphs) and (b) in the conclusion (say two to four paragraphs), and (c) it is of general interest (e.g. on studying or note-taking or answering examination questions, etc.).

Developing a Card Index System

In addition it may be helpful to give students some guidance on developing their own information storage system. It must be made quite clear to students that a card system is *not* a learning process or even a substitute for one.

There is a variety of card systems. The cheapest to operate involves using key words (a Thesaurus for the discipline(s) involved may help). Students could be advised to use key words on indexing cards (see below). In addition there are alphabetical indexing cards for author names. As each paper or book is summarised on the cards (using linear or patterned notes) the card is numbered in sequence. The card should be headed in a standard form; examples are shown below. The summary is related to the key words and listed under each appropriate key word. It may be helpful to run one or two specific sessions to encourage students to compare techniques and to try the system. There is a variety of card sizes available. I find 15 cm × 10 cm (6 × 4 ins) most useful.

Examples of Information on Cards

Data cards

216

Harris, N.D.C. (1979)   London, Croom Helm
PREPARING EDUCATIONAL MATERIALS

217

Morgan, A.S. (1976)   Studies in Higher Education 1 (1) 63-8
LEARNING THROUGH PROJECTS

Keyword card (using two sets of data above)

LEARNING   216
           217

Alphabetical card

M   Morgan, A.S.   217

Examinations

Syndicate groups are an ideal method for revising for examinations. Here students devise questions based on past papers (with expected answers) which other members of the group attempt. In this way students learn more about the types of questions set, what other people consider important parts and how different people interpret the same question. At the same time the very preparation of questions and answers is excellent revision.

To take this idea a stage further, syndicate learning could be used in a final year course to devise, work out questions for, and write the answers to 'examinations'. It is possible that syndicates of learners could by this means develop a broader understanding of the course than many individual learners.

Many students, while at school, were given guidelines in answering questions beginning 'discuss', 'describe', etc. In continuing and higher education, where generally no such help is forthcoming, some comparison of the interpretation of questions by other students would be useful.

Summary of a Suggested Routine for Helping Students to Interpret Examination Questions (Based on Gibbs, 1976)

1. Give students a typical examination question starting with the word 'discuss' or 'describe' or 'evaluate' or 'compare'.
2. Ask students to spend 5 minutes writing down the sort of way in which they would expect to answer the question.
3. Ask pairs of students to look for differences in their way of answering (about 5–10 minutes).
4. Ask groups of four students to attempt to find a consensus view (about 10–15 minutes).
5. Ask groups to report back on the best outline and any disagreements.
6. How do their expectations relate to yours?

This is an *active* learning exercise for students with the lecturer acting as organiser or manager. By such an exercise the students learn much more about what is required from examination questions than simply by reading them.

When past questions are available they should also include information such as examiner's criticisms of answers and suggested content, since the questions themselves can be of little value.

The purpose of examination questions will be dealt with in more detail in Chapter 6. However for most end-of-course examinations the questions are there for one of two purposes — (a) to discriminate between students to enable classification, and (b) to measure whether students have mastered the learning — although both ideas are seldom achieved in one examination or more particularly in one question. In examination work the student gets no specific information back on his work, purely a global mark. The examination plays no useful part in learning. Thus a considerable amount of effort has been expended from which the student or learner derives little useful information.

Some interesting innovations in examinations have occurred

recently. In one case (Good, 1978) students were given the opportunity to be present for 20-25 minutes whilst their script was marked. Here discussion took place between the examiner and the student. If the student was not satisfied he could ask to be marked by a different examiner. 95 per cent of the students availed themselves of this opportunity to be present at the marking and less than 5 percent asked for a re-appraisal. Therefore it can be said that an excellent use of examinations is to give an opportunity for a discussion of a particular problem area between lecturer and student. It also enables students to form a clearer idea of what is required. In another example (Redfern, 1978) students were told the specific purpose of an examination and given a practice run before the actual examination. If the examination is to be a worthwhile part of the learning experience its purpose should be explicit. There is no reason why the student be put in a position of ignorance with regard to the purpose of the assessment (Klug, 1977).

Learning to Solve Problems

The ultimate in solving problems is to be given a problem, to select the right questions to ask and to endeavour to answer those questions. Methods of problem-solving are sometimes called lateral thinking (de Bono, 1970), divergent thinking (e.g. Hudson, 1966), or simply flexibility in thinking. Whilst flexibility may come more naturally to some students than others, there is no evidence to suggest that flexibility cannot be developed. To assist students in developing flexibility one technique is to give them a simple problem, for example the writing of an essay. The essay lends itself more easily to the technique than numerical type problems.

A Suggested Routine for Essay Writing Exercises (After Gibbs, 1976)

1. Give students a title for an essay — or ask them to use the title of one they have had recently.
2. Ask them to start writing an answer using their own method (allow about 5 minutes).
3. Stop them and ask them to start again with a totally different bias (allow about 5 minutes).
4. Stop them writing and repeat step 3.
5. Divide them up into pairs to discuss what they have done and why (say 5–10 minutes).
6. Make up groups of four to look for any clues to ways of finding different methods (5–10 minutes).

7. Give the students opportunities to make two further attempts of 5 minutes each.

A simple exercise such as this can be far more effective than just telling them how to do it. Students should realise that they can write in more than one way. It is important to emphasise in de-briefing that there are various methods which one can try and the first chosen may not necessarily be the best for the topic.

Having developed some idea of flexible thinking the next stage is less difficult. Ask students, given a problem to be solved, to write down all possible questions that could be asked. A scoring technique to encourage original relevant questions could be used (e.g. with 25 students, if a question is asked by all, 1 point; if only by 5, 5 points; if by 1, 25 points).

Exercises of this kind need a lot of careful management, for they can generate insecurity for both lecturer and learners, and therefore the whole exercise must be a co-operative venture in learning. Taking down copious notes about facts and figures may be a more secure form of learning for the lecturer, but is still very insecure for many students.

Creativity

Solving problems is part of the way to creativity. In higher and continuing education students are often set quite large problems in the form of projects, presentations or dissertations. The student is required to demonstrate that he is capable of not only working on his own, but also doing something different or original (Adderley *et al.*, 1975; Dowdeswell and Harris, 1979).

The project or dissertation is used both as a learning and as an assessment device and because of this presents the student with a considerable problem. The project or dissertation requires a great deal of time and energy, with no clear information or feedback on progress, and at the end it may be assessed subjectively by methods which are kept secret from the student. In some disciplines (for example, architecture and fine art) this type of work is the principal method of assessment.

A variety of methods has been attempted to rationalise learning and assessment procedures. The idea of a contract between the student and the lecturer has some merit. In this the two agree, prior to the start of the creative work, what the requirements should be and what constraints are involved. These can be committed to paper and signed by both parties as a form of contract. Any changes have to be agreed by both parties. Obviously this sort of procedure is more satisfactory from an assessment point of view, but danger can lie in poor leadership.

Some new universities, for example, Roskelde in Denmark and Bremen in W. Germany (see Cornwall, 1975), had their whole course structure designed originally around project learning. In the case of Bremen problems arose because other universities and the bureaucratic establishment were unwilling to accept the qualifications. Whilst the basic idea has been preserved, certain disciplines (e.g. physics) have fallen back on more conventional teaching in parallel with project teaching.

Discovery Learning

Heuristic or discovery learning is the name given to the problem-solving approach. Instead of the learner being given all the concepts and principles which he should apply in a new situation, the situations are given and the learner looks for patterns, ideas and principles. There have been many writers who have advocated these ideas (for example Wertheimer, 1943 and Katona, 1940). The basic argument here is that problem-solving is not generally the application of known principles but an attempt to use flexible and original paths of ideas. Experiments carried out by Wertheimer and Katona showed that by training or education based on problem-solving of this kind the student was able to develop in a creative way. Similar principles have been used in many aspects of primary education for years.

In secondary education discovery learning often became guided discovery learning, particularly in the science disciplines. The 'discovery' was acceptable provided it led to the orthodox tradition. One big problem arose because, whereas the didactic method of teaching had built-in regular checks of progress, in the guided discovery approach these were more obscure. Neither the teacher nor the learner was quite sure whether the previous learning could or could not be assumed.

In order to enable students to carry out guided discovery, a large bank of materials or resources is needed — booklets, study packs (e.g. off-prints collected into a wallet), equipment, apparatus for science-based subjects, stored materials (audio tape, video tape, microfiche) — which provide a base from which the learner can 'discover'. Often, however, the learner is not expected to go outside these resources. This type of learning environment is sometimes called resource-based learning.

Means v. Ends Approaches

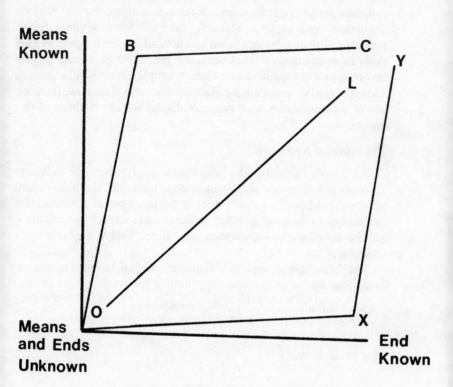

Means Known

B

C

Y

L

O

X

Means and Ends Unknown

End Known

A simple model of learning (MacDonald-Ross, 1973) suggests that discovery approach as being OBC, the guided discovery is nearer OL.

Other techniques used to encourage problem-solving include simulation and gaming. Students take on roles within a game prescribed by the rules laid down by the organiser or designer. Within these rules and the resources provided, the player or student may be involved in a competitive exercise. A simple example of a game is Monopoly, a complex one the Harvard Business Game involving the use of a computer. A wide range of disciplines use methods of this nature.

Behavioural Approach

Many people think that the behavioural approach is the only one associated with educational technology. Certainly the behavioural approach has been the basis of much of the development of educational technology to date, but as other evidence and research accumulate it will be necessary to incorporate new ideas. Technology is always changing.

The behavioural approach depends on two simple models, a biological one:

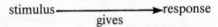

or a physical one:

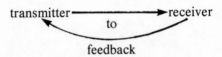

In the biological model a question is, for instance, a form of stimulus requiring the response of an answer, whereas the physical model is the teacher transmitting the question to the learner who feeds back with the answer. In order to operate this approach it is essential to know where one is going; thus from this system, behavioural objectives have expectations of

(1) performance from the learner;
(2) a specified level of performance;
(3) certain conditions under which the performance will take place (Mager, 1957; Miller, 1970).

Based on the traditional orthodoxy of disciplines it is relatively easy for the lecturer to specify what he expects of a student. Often the easiest way of doing this is to write down the sort of questions a student would be expected to answer on completion of learning. Indeed for learning of factual information or for skills of manipulation the specification can be very explicit, but the more originality is expected, the more difficult the specification. On the means/end model the behavioural approach is line OXY (see page 31).

The original learning method associated with educational technology was the small step, programmed learning approach. Each element of behavioural change was carefully planned in a logical sequence and evidence of learning was carefully monitored. Initial successes were very high. However the protagonists approached programmed learning as *the* method of learning rather than as *a* method. The analytical work involved in preparing a programme was great and the programmes needed considerable use as well as success to warrant the investment of time, people and other resources.

However the highly systematic approach to learning has continued in educational technology. The less detailed programme has evolved into the form of work cards or work-sheets with stated objectives. Associated with the work-sheets and the work cards are various materials and resources, and the learner may be required to do some specified reading. This type of learning is often called resource-based learning (line OL; see page 31).

It is interesting to note that two apparently extreme points of view on learning psychology, when applied by developers of educational materials, have ended up giving very similar positions. This is in the use of resource materials for students' own study.

Learning to Use Non-Print Media

As has been shown in the previous two sections, resource-based learning incorporates media other than print. These media will include actual objects, displays, drawings, diagrams. They may well also include audio recordings, video recordings, audio recordings synchronised with visual displays and film. Relatively little is known about learning from audio visual media.

There seems to be no reason why passive learning from audio visual media should be any more effective than passive learning in other situations. However before elaborating on this idea it is worth comparing some elements of audio visual media with the printed medium. The printed medium inevitably has a linear aspect to it because the eye scans linearly (even very fast readers who scan diagonally are following a linear sequence). The whole assembly print is in a linear format. Most Western thought has been communicated through print, so traditional structures have tended to be linear. The printed medium has a further dimension, that of delay, since it is very difficult to present printed materials instantaneously.

If McLuhan (1964) is to be believed, television has a very different characteristic, that of immediacy and of mosaic format. Do our students, with their long hours of television viewing behind them, have different thought patterns from us? Do they have a more pictorial thought pattern than we do? Is this in any way related to the success of art forms in communicating with ordinary people?

Printed material is highly visual. However the visual element is nearer to sequential than holist (or haptic rather than visual; page 17).

Television has often been used to present lectures for passive viewing. These presentations make little use of the medium as such. The lecture, although an audio and visual format, is not a television format. Television is a dynamic visual medium. It has the potential for a high degree of involvement and the most successful uses of television in formal learning institutions have been:

(1) for replay of human interactions within the group of students who are viewing;
(2) in presentation of visual material for analysis;
(3) in presenting ideas and materials which are not accessible to students within their own institution.

To date the involvement of students in productions has been minimal, and yet what a powerful learning medium it is. The student can consider the communication potential of this medium and endeavour to express himself through it. He can take on the presenter's role or a more technical role such as cameraman.

How can one present ideas and information to others unless one has a clear understanding oneself? An interesting simple example is provided by a small final year class of sixteen students. Until 1976 these students were each required to present a half-hour seminar on a recent research paper in their discipline. Now they are split into two groups of eight. Each group of eight is expected to present a simple television presentation on two or three related research papers. The programme is limited in length to twenty minutes. Only photographs, diagrams and the presenters themselves are permitted in the production. The six hours of formal studio work, in addition to the preparation of material to communicate, is a battle for time and comprehension, bearing in mind especially that the other group and some lecturers will be viewing the presentation critically.

The use of audio visual materials for self-instruction is in its infancy. Materials which are successful for a group interaction may not be suitable for individual viewing. It is interesting to note that where the option is provided group viewing is more popular than individual viewing (Harris and Kirkhope, 1977). Is this an example of the syndicate learning group occurring naturally? Is it an example of the heavy involvement effect of television viewing? The group of students cited often talked to one another during the actual playback, they switched off and discussed, they rewound the tape to check their impressions.

Similarly it has been found (Buckingham and Jones, 1976) that for the use of synchronised audio tape with 35 mm slides, a pair of students working together is more efficient and more satisfying to each person than individual viewing.

The idea of printed material associated with audio visual material will be elaborated in Chapter 9.

Learning to Use the Modern Library

The use of non-book media in the library can actually be used as a means of persuading students to use printed materials. A small group (about eight) of engineering students were asked to view an experiment shown on television from which they recorded the readings. The experiment, which took over three hours to set up and obtain a limited number of readings, was shown in fifteen minutes (this included a brief theoretical resumé) and the students were asked to draw conclusions from the readings. The group was then subdivided, one half going to compare their data with that provided by manufacturers of similar equipment, whilst the other searched journals for research reports on the equipment. The whole group met their tutor two hours later to discuss their findings. In this way the tutor was able to meet several groups who had been involved in a learning experience. The evidence from the students suggested that they remembered this experience above many other learning experiences and that for many of them it was the first time that they had been required to use the library, as opposed to making use of it as a base for carrying out their work.

It is often assumed that one of the attributes of a graduate is that he will know how to find his way round the literature of his discipline. The student is usually left to his own devices in developing this skill. In recent years librarians have become very aware of the need for user education. Unfortunately much of their effort has been in isolation, so that exercises in using libraries are divorced from the discipline itself. Only when the student sees the need for using a library (e.g. when preparing a dissertation or a project) do these user education programmes have real relevance.

A more satisfactory approach would be a collaborative effort between librarians and lecturers. Students are often provided with a vast book list, bibliography or reading list, but are given little guidance on their use. Whilst it is clear that a student should find a text most suitable to his learning style, but compatible with the lecturers' expectations, nevertheless some guidance is useful. By the final year of a degree course, a student should know not only the standard reference material (be it Marx, Chomsky, Kung, or a standard text book in a science or engineering discipline), but also what journals have what kind of papers, what bibliographies, abstracting journals and other facilities are available.

The figure below makes tentative suggestions for a possible framework on the development of skills during a course to take account of this.

The figure is obviously simplified, but by the end of each course the student should have (a) a set of basic or standard text references, (b) a set of fringe texts, (c) a set of basic or standard journal references and their location. in addition he should have knowledge of a set of basic or standard abstracting systems and methods of information retrieval. The range is determined according the student needs — obviously an engineer has a different need from, say, a lawyer.

Methods of approach need to be systematic and related to expectations, assignments and examinations or other forms of assessment. The course materials need to be designed so that information retrieval is a challenge at each stage for the student, with some repetitions for reinforcement and retention of learning.

One possible method is to use regular work-sheets throughout the course with a gradual development of requirement as in the figure. For example early work-sheets could lay the whole thing out with reference to specified texts, later ones would give less and less specific references leading to final year dissertations or projects. Early references to papers could be done by gathering off-prints collected into a study pack, preferably giving more than one point of view. At a

Development of Information Access and Retrieval Skills

FIRST
YEAR

Texts chapter and verse
Literature search in
limited domain of texts.
Select own references.

Journals specified articles
(e.g. study pack)
Literature search in limited
domain of texts.
Select own references.

Abstract journals
Specified search in limited
number.
Literature search in specified
area(s).
Select own references.

FINAL YEAR

later stage a similar method might be used for retrieval systems such as bibliographies, abstracting journals or 'current contents'. The systematic development of information retrieval techniques is an essential part of any undergraduate course and of increasing importance as the bank of available knowledge increases.

4 LEVELS OF LEARNING

Ultimate Learning

What should a learner expect to get from his learning? This will obviously vary from course to course and with the level of education. However examinations, projects, dissertations, extended essays, and the production of original artifacts are all examples of the products of his learning. Thus learning is shown by some kind of performance or presentation. On the basis of this some grading or mark will be allocted towards the final mark for classification.

The current interest in creative work may be a reflection of the recognition of a need to turn our attention to problem-solving rather than repetition of subject matter. Project work is one example of the problem-solving approach. The tradition of projects is of greater standing in courses such as architecture. Examples of learning purposes related to design projects are:

(1) *'to confirm and apply knowledge'* by creating novel situations in which the student's newly acquired knowledge can be applied and its further relevance understood;

(2) *'to develop knowledge'* by causing the student with a problem to demand knowledge in advance of his present level and to make the search for knowledge a part of his search for a solution;

(3) *'to relate areas of knowledge'* by making the student consider combining various aspects of his knowledge and develop skill in the manipulation and co-ordination of the whole body of experience. (Morgan, 1976)

In order to achieve these learning aspirations other elements are involved too. It is difficult to persuade students to carry out this work unless they are motivated. The motivation element is often an important aspect of project work to students. Students often claim that the project is one of the few pieces of work in which they have 'got really involved' (Miller and Parlett, 1974).

The use of projects and discovery learning for these purposes is nothing new. These ideas have been advocated by psychologists of the gestalt school and by those who emphasise process rather than outcome, for example Bruner (1960). However the ideas are not limited to the creative arts, for they are applicable across all subjects at all levels. As I stated in Chapter 3, some institutions have devised their whole course structures around project learning. Bearing in mind the different styles of learners (see Chapter 2), projects as the main base for learning may be unreasonable in all institutions. Nevertheless project learning is considered by most educationalists to be an important learning area, whether it is the basis of a course or only part of the final year of the course.

Resource Problems

Perhaps the largest constraint on the use of project-type work on a wider basis is a lack of suitable resource material, but there are many other questions. If each student is to do an individual project where is the space? Where are the materials? Where are the books? How can adequate tutorial adivce be provided? How can an adequate check on progress be made? Many of these questions make assumptions about existing use of space, materials, library books, tutorial advice and assessment procedures. Are these assumptions reasonable? Do existing methods really provide the best possible learning for students? Many of these questions are largely related to factors of management and the organisation of learning.

There is remarkably little material published about the use of space for projects. However it is clear that subjects such as architecture which are heavily project-biased, have a large proportion of their floor space set aside as 'studios' primarily for project type work. In these spaces students can leave their work, knowing that the space will not be used for other purposes.

In the Physics Department at Bristol University it was found that about £25 per student was spent on final year project work (at 1973/4 prices). In addition a general expenditure of up to £1,500 was spent on specialised equipment for a total of eighty students and one thousand hours of workshop time (in addition to technicians' time in the laboratories). Bearing in mind the level of student fees, this is hardly a large expenditure (Mansell, 1975).

The shortage of books in a library is more often associated with students wanting the same book at the same time rather than different students wanting different books. The problem for projects may be that the required books are not available in the library. The usual way of overcoming this problem is to reduce the scope of the projects to fit the resources.

Tutorial advice for projects can often only be available at the expense of other methods of teaching and learning. The decision on use of staff involves a judgement of the relative values of the educational experiences and also depends on the purposes of learning (see Chapter 5).

Projects and dissertations are notoriously difficult to assess. Is the assessment on a comparative basis between students, is it an assessment of performance, or or learning? Some attempts have been made to have an agreed contract of expectations between students and lecturer on projects (Black, 1975). The assessment of the project is based on the contract or expectations which can only be altered by agreement of both parties. Assessment often puts a damper on projects, particularly when the assessment is primarily associated with the written report. Clearly communication of the project by a written report is a key element, but is it the only element? (Dowdeswell and Harris, 1979; Adderley *et al*, 1975.)

Rational Build-Up

Because of these problems, projects and dissertations are often limited to the first and third purposes outlined on page 39, namely 'to confirm and apply knowledge' and 'to relate areas of knowledge', and sometimes even to the first purpose only. Thus the knowlege bank can be built up prior to the project and the student is only required to carry out a pre-specified project in order to show his ability in applying knowledge.

This rational build-up gives more control to the lecturer and enables existing methods of teaching and learning to be continued as long as possible. Is this convenience of administration and management so important that it takes precedence over the learning experience?

The overall design of projects requires many decisions to be made, not least being those concerned with the constraints. The administration and management of projects are the key preparations for their smooth running.

Many Pre-Requisites

Whichever method is used for introducing the project or dissertation there are many requirements from the student. In a course based on project work the student needs to feel that he is able to cope in this learning environment. For him it may be an insecure learning environment, as it involves extensive preparation and groundwork. During the creative process there is little opportunity to check one's progress because of one's own involvement. Considerable drive, enthusiasm and a holist approach are essential in the student. How often is any screening of students carried out to look for such factors when selecting them for such a course? The switch to a project or dissertation at the end of the course requires both a change in roles and a change in expectations from staff and students coupled by a change in learning techniques. In some courses there is a change from a heavily teacher-dependent course, with students expected to agree with the points of view of the lecturer and the tenets of the discipline, to the opposite; a student-dependent course requiring originality and creativity, which is completely at conflict with the demands implicit in the former. It is hardly surprising that in these cases the assessments of projects often correlate poorly with conventional examination.

Is it possible to make the transition less dramatic? How vital is the bank of knowledge gained prior to learning of the project kind? Is it possible to train students in the project type of work? Is project work vastly different from problem-solving? The answers to these questions determine the learning strategy. There are no 'correct' answers.

Vast Knowledge Bank

The rate of increase of knowledge is such that it doubles once about every seven years. Not only is it no longer reasonable to find a learned person whose knowledge spans many disciplines, it is also unreasonable to expect a student to have other than a relatively small knowledge span in one discipline. At secondary school level there is much talk of a core curriculum. A special Assessment of Performance Unit has been set up by the Department of Education and Science to specify the core elements in which a certain standard is expected. In certain disciplines which have strong professional bodies (particularly those which are in control of professional qualifications essential to employment), considerable control is exerted on the core curriculum in continuing and higher education.

The vast expansion of available knowledge also poses different problems. As has previously been stated, it is unreasonable to expect a vast storage of information in the brain. It is more reasonable to expect one to have the knowledge of how and where to access the knowledge quickly. It has been clear for decades now that storage of all available information is beyond human capacity. None of us in our work depends exclusively on our own knowledge store; we have immediate access to a limited store in our range of personal books and journals, and an extended store in the information system associated with libraries. Materials, knowledge, definitions, theories can change rapidly, making our own store more obsolete. Whether you are a plumber, an electrician, an engineer or a social worker, there is a need to be able to update your store of knowledge continuously. It should be made quite clear in educational materials that knowledge and theories can change rapidly.

The information system continues to become more complex, thus in order to access the required information it becomes increasingly important to identify the correct question or to find alternative key words. For example when using an index of a book the reader is very dependent upon finding the key words associated with that particular index, yet how many courses consider information access as a serious element? The whole basis of project work is highly dependent on this ability to access information.

The basis of information access is still assumed to be heavily oriented to the historical unified systems of problem-solving associated with disciplines. The continuous learning of conceptual frameworks associated with disciplines ensures the continuation of that discipline but can have a blinkering effect on students. In the past traditional problem-solving techniques may have been relevant in a society where change was slow, but in a rapidly changing society there is an ever-increasing need to use new problem-solving techniques whatever their origin. There is a balance between the extremes of standard problem-solving methods and untried methods, but only in some of the newer study areas such as management is there much evidence of the use of a variety of problem-solving approaches.

Existing Hierarchies of Learning

Much of the existing work on hierarchies of learning is associated with the basic assumptions of (a) a disciplinary approach, (b) a rational build-up of knowledge and theories. Based on these two assumptions, the two systems most widely known are those of Bloom and his co-workers and that of Gagne. Both have their origins in the United States of America and have behavioural connotations.

Bloom and his co-workers suggested that there were three basic domains or areas of learning:

1. Cognitive learning — mental skills and abilities which students are expected to acquire.
2. Affective learning — attitudes.
3. Psychomotor learning — physical skills and abilities which students are expected to acquire.

Relationships between Cognitive and Affective Domains of Learning

Cognitive Domain	Affective Domain
Knowledge	Attending
Comprehension	Responding
Application	Valuing
Analysis	Organisation of a Value System
Synthesis	Characterisation by a Value
Evaluation	

Examples of the terms shown are as follows:

Knowledge: terminology, facts, conventions, methods.

Comprehension: translation of verbal to symbolic, interpretation, extrapolation, determining consequences and effects.

Application: use of abstractions such as rules of procedures, technical principles, ideas in particular and concrete situations.

Analysis: breaking down a communication into its constituent parts, recognition of unstated assumptions, distinguishing facts and hypotheses.

Synthesis: ability to propose ways of testing hypotheses.

Evaluation: making judgements about materials by criteria within or external to the material.

Attending: willing to receive or attend to.

Responding: develops awareness of aesthetic factors, willingness to be of service, develops a keen interest in, enjoyment of.

Valuing: assumes responsibility for, assumes an active role in, faith in power of reason, devotion to ideas and ideals.

Organisation of Value System: forms judgements as to the responsibility of individuals, begins to form judgements concerning the type of life he wants to lead.

Characterisation by a Value: the habit of approaching objectively, relies increasingly on the method of science in finding answers about society and the world, confidence in ability to succeed, develops a conscience, develops a consistent philosophy of life.

They consider the three domains to be interlinked (Bloom, 1956, Krathwohl, 1964). The purpose of the classification, or taxonomy, is to enable teachers to communicate better with one another. It has already been made clear that there is a relationship between motivation and learning and by positioning the main levels alongside one another some discussion on this relationship can be carried out.

The authors derived their taxonomies by analysing extensive information provided by lecturers and colleges on the purposes of their courses. In two handbooks, one on the cognitive and the other on the affective domain, they give detailed taxonomies but point out that they have reservations on the order of presentation. The table below shows the relationship between the cognitive and affective domains of learning.

There seems to be an expectation of high affective levels associated with a high cognitive level and vice versa. Despite criticisms of these hierarchies, they have been widely used and have been effective in bringing about communication between teachers and learners. With regard to a definitive hierarchy there is much room for doubt, but the main levels shown have been found most useful at all levels of education as a basis for communication for design of learning and assessment.

How do these levels relate to the ideas of projects and problem solving? Synthesis and evaluation should emerge from most project work. Problem solving can be at any of the levels from application upwards. A hierarchy in the psychomotor domain has been published (Harrow, 1972). The levels in this are shown below:

1. Reflex movements (to flex, to relax).
2. Basic fundamental movements (to walk, to grasp).
3. Perceptual abilities (to write, to distinguish by touch).
4. Physical abilities (to endure, to move precisely).
5. Skilled movements (to type, to change or modify basic movement patterns).
6. Non-discursive communication (to express facially, perform skilfully).

Most work has been associated with the cognitive domain, sometimes to the exclusion of the others. It must be stressed that there is an interrelationship probably amounting to considerable overlap between these three domains. Much of examining in continuing and higher education is associated with levels 1,2, and 3 in the cognitive domain. Examinations often determine what students learn and how lecturers teach, and this will be dealt with in Chapter 6.

Gagné (1970) suggests five domains of learning: motor skills, verbal information, intellectual skills, cognitive strategies and attitudes. Motor skills such as writing, typing, using equipment, and playing instruments need practice and this is the main characteristic of this domain. He suggests that verbal information (i.e. facts, principles and generalisations) consitute the need for continued learning in a particular subject area. The term 'knowledge' is usually used to denote this and the evidence suggests the need for an organised meaningful context. Gagné (1970) is probably best known for his work on intellectual skills. He lists discriminations, concepts and rules as the basic skills, leading to development of higher principles (one's own development of rules) which are heavily dependent on the learning of pre-requisite skills. The cognitive strategies are primarily aimed at self-management in learning, remembering and thinking — what has been referred to as 'problem-solving' and 'learning to learn' in this book. The domain of attitudes in Gagné's work matches the affective domain quite closely.

Conflicts between Learning Patterns and Learning Methods

Description of Learning	Learner Action
Using other people's learning	Repetition
Organised learning	Solving problems provided
Learning to learn (A)	Solving own problems
Learning to learn (B)	Setting up own problems

Consider two examples: a sequential converger (see p. 17) relating to project work and a holist diverger relating to a conventional lecture and problems-class approach. The sequential converger is self-motivated to continue his own learning strategy (e.g. solving problems provided). His learning pattern is associated with the first two rows of the table. Project work requires him to set up his own problems (learning to learn (B)). External motivation may be necessary to encourage this type of learner even to attempt an alien strategy. A simple motivation could be the allocation of marks for the project, although this would not work for all students.

Similarly, the holist diverger is self-motivated to set up his own problems (learning to learn (B)). His learning pattern is associated with the last two rows of the table. He may require external motivation to take on the learning style of repetition followed by solving problems provided. The conventional examination may act as such motivation for some students. These simple examples emphasise (a) the problems of some learning methods for students with a particular learning pattern, and (b) the problems that a student's learning pattern may present for some learning methods. There is no right or wrong approach because students may use a combination of both. It is interesting to note that in many disciplines, the discipline base matches one style of learner rather than the other.

Media and Access to Information

The media, especially the more technological media such as television and computers, are relatively new technologies and we have not yet realised their potential or reorganised our strategies and conceptual frameworks to incorporate them. They are still at the stage where we view them like the 'horseless carriage' rather than the 'car', or as the 'wire-less' rather than 'radio' (McLuhan, 1964). 'Television' and 'computer' may be words rather like 'horseless carriage' and 'wire-less' which will become obsolete when a fuller realisation of their relationship with our environment is realised.

Television and computers may well ultimately bring about complete revisions in our conceptions of learning, which are at present heavily print-oriented. At present television is only gradually developing from being a new form of film, and computers are changing slowly from being a rapid form of calculation.

In the long term it is certain that these and other new media will cause considerable changes in our concept of education. The bases of education may be information science, cybernetics and communications technology rather than psychology and programmed learning (if those ever were the bases of education!). At present we are only beginning to find the potential of television and computers in learning, so they are used as adjuncts to existing learning strategies (Hooper, 1977). The advent of microprocessing may accelerate the change in the meaning of learning. As access to information becomes much easier (Gosling, 1978), so the processing and selection of information will become keys to learning.

5 PURPOSES OF LEARNING

What Is Education?

An immediate problem associated with the institutionalisation of education is the feeling that it is something which only takes place in particular buildings at a certain time of one's life. The correspondence colleges, the National Extension College and the Open University are examples of institutions which have attempted to break down this artificial restriction. The mass media have great potential for breaking down the impression that education is associated with buildings or particular ages.

Education is not something which tries to make each individual into a neat package to fit the existing needs of society. Education should provide the opportunity to cope with the unknown future with its changes in jobs, changes in transport and changes in mobility.

It is difficult to look into the future, but certain patterns do seem to be emerging. Some of these patterns have been alluded to in previous chapters: the rapid expansion of information, the changing patterns of communication, the increasing need to develop search strategies, the questioning of the orthodox approach.

Forming a philosophy of life and developing a series of interests and activities for leisure are important elements of a learner's self-development. An interesting student suggestion was that involvement in sporting activities, in other student societies or even in student politics should be taken into account when deciding on borderline cases in degree classification (Educational Services Bulletin, 1977). For many employers the evidence of a wide range of interests is as important as the level of qualification (Cox and Collins, 1975).

The rapid increase in the numbers of adult learners has affected the requirements of courses. Adult students have pragmatic reasons for undertaking further education: to enable them to change job or roles, to enable them to improve their performance in their existing job or role, to develop an interest (i.e. an outside or leisure activity), or simply to improve on past performance. Adult learners may either lack an appreciation of the need for a learning strategy or never even have considered it.

48

Learning to Learn

Whatever the level of education, one of the primay purposes of education should be to enable the learner to learn on his own. One of the important elements of learning to learn is to find out more about oneself. What note-taking techniques are better (e.g. linear or patterned)? What hours of the day are the best times for working? What are the best methods for solving problems; intuitive or systematic? Most students have been given little opportunity to find answers to these questions. Surely part of preparing learning experiences is the provision of opportunity to try out methods. An informal method with mixed disciplinary groups is suggested in a very worthwhile booklet *Learning to Study* (Gibbs, 1976). The system advocated is based on individuals writing their own ideas or answers to questions on the topic under discussion, then grouping into pairs for comparative purposes and, finally, working in groups for consensus. Each session lasts 60 to 90 minutes with the possibility of feedback at the end. A group of up to fifty students at a time can be involved in this kind of work. (Examples are given in Chapter 3.) The discussions within pairs and fours are sometimes called buzz groups (Bligh, 1972).

Certain elements of learning to learn involve working on one's own, such as taking notes from lectures, books or journals. This is not to eliminate the opportunity to compare with others. It is as well to learn that notes should be viewed very early after writing them, for evidence suggests a rapid fall in retention (Bligh, 1972); last-minute work for examinations becomes first vision not revision. Looking at notes soon after writing them may be an advantage as a syndicate activity by a small informal group of students rather than as a formal or tutorial group. The lecturer can give help within a sixty-minute period by providing two short breaks, one in the middle and one near the end when he requires students to read the notes that they have written (Howe, 1977). Within present discipline structures it is important that the student has a clear grasp of overall problem-solving strategies. These strategies are gleaned, with luck, by attendance at a host of different lecture courses. Perhaps a more efficient method could be to spend some time during the overall course on problem-solving strategies, the remaining lecture courses or classes emphasising the application of those strategies. Some disciplines appear to be intuitively based, others systematically based — few are either specifically one or the other. The access to resources and materials has already been outlined in Chapter 3.

Certainly students need to know means of accessing appropriate materials, whether they are in print or other media. The questions they need answered are:

1. Where are they kept?
2. How do I ask for them?
3. Where can I find what materials are available?
4. To whom can I go for help, now while studying and in 5 years?

Obviously these activities will be collaborative ones with librarians, who are being recognised more and more as people who provide access to resources to help users, rather than as guardians of books. With the increasing use of microfiche catalogues and possibly the use of PRESTEL, the familiar card index drawers will become less and less common. Library stock in all media will be computer stored. At present the easiest format for multiple access is probably microfiche, closely followed by displays on television screens. It may soon be possible to access much British and European literature through PRESTEL, the Post Office alphanumeric and visual display system. This system has vastly more potential for education than Cefax or Oracle, the equivalent display systems using the television broadcast channels, because of its much larger storage and access capacity. Perhaps PRESTEL is the potential educational television channel; only time will tell. Costs at present put it outside the range of the individual user, although not by much at £400 per annum rental (1977 quoted price). The interface with information systems is going to be the key to future education. Is the role going to be taken by present librarians or by teachers? Is the role going to be seen essentially as a source to enable the user to learn to use the system himself, or as part of the role of a jealously guarded profession which endeavours to ensure its own future by insisting that the intermediary must always be used? Access to information is important in problem-solving.

Problem-Solving Techniques

The basis of problem-solving has been discussed in Chapter 4. Problem-solving is a learner-based activity, not a passive reception of existing techniques. A student does not learn to solve a problem by watching the lecturer solve it, he at best remembers certain elements or at worst can repeat the identical solution. The idea of verbatim and non-verbatim learning has been elaborated by Marton (1975) and his co-workers in Sweden. Certain techniques for the preparation of educational materials have been reported as very successful. One such technique is called mathemagenics (Rothkopf, 1972). This technique consists of interposing questions within sections of text:

| text section | T_1 | T_2 | T_3 |
| associated question | Q_1 | Q_2 | Q_3 |

These questions are either preview or review questions. At the end of the text chapter is a set of questions based on those in the text.

Marton (1975) and his co-workers used the same techniques in courses in economics and education. They found that review questions were more effective than no questions, which in turn were more effective than preview questions. In addition they found that, when asking for in-depth understanding, students with no questions performed better than those with specific questions and than those with content neutral statements.

The idea of efficiency of learning has been primarily applied to accumulated knowledge (sometimes called surface learning). There is no attempt at problem-solving in any of these sorts of ideas. These are discipline-related strategies in order to accumulate knowledge. Processing of knowledge is needed for the future, not accumulation of knowledge. It is clear that students need to have problem-solving techniques which have previously been used and elaborated — the starting point for conventional learning. What is not clear is the best sequence of learning. Should not problem-solving exercises (e.g. projects) be running parallel with the previous methods used, rather than in sequence?

Problem-solving does not only involve asking questions but finding routes and deriving conclusions which are carefully reported together with their limitations and the assumptions on which the solution is derived. An interesting example is an examination in pharmacology outlined in Chapter 6, where students are given the data from a research paper and required to derive a conclusion and the assumptions on which that conclusion is made.

One Russian writer (Landa, 1974) argues that many problems can be solved by algorithmic or pseudo-algorithmic methods (i.e. where certain assumptions are made). he suggests that all students should learn algorithmic methods and that they should derive *their own* algorithmic solutions to problems. He stresses that the student should *not* just learn an algorithmic solution, but derive his own, which may well be different from anyone else's. Irrespective of whether one agrees with the general use of algorithmic methods, the premiss of requiring students to use that method while deriving their own solutions is the key to problem-solving methods. Algorithms are but one of many possible routing methods.

In learning based on disciplines the problem-solving methods are often presented in a variety of contexts, when the overall strategy may well be better used by students in different contexts. For example, in physics, flow theory is often presented in heat flow, fluid flow and electrical flow, while in each area field theory is also applicable along with magnetism and gravity. The present method of teaching uses one strategy; the facts are presented, then followed by simple theories which lead to simple problem-solving. Perhaps more emphasis on the generalised problem-solving technique and less on the detail of the variety of applications may be a step in the right direction.

Just how much specialised vocabulary (jargon), used to convey exact meanings to other specialists, is necessary? How much sophisticated theory is necessary? In today's world the jargon is necessary to communicate with other specialists and one of our problems is the difficulty of communication between speicalists and non-specialists. A clear requirement in any learning situation is the need to be able to communicate orally and in writing to non-specialists.

Communication Techniques

Most experts, other than those working in specialised research will spend a large proportion of their working life communicating with non-experts, convincing them, informing them, or briefing them. This communication will be either orally or in writing. In spite of the emphasis on the written word in education little attention is paid to writing for the non-specialist, and such communication techniques are ignored in most courses.

Enthusiasm often has an influence on communication. A learner not only derives enthusiasm from his own ability to learn, but also from the aesthetic appreciation of the area of study. Many solutions to problems are of aesthetic value in their own right. Aesthetic sense in students is often brought out by the enthusiasm of the lecturer. Surely education is not to become so mechanistic that this sense is lost! This aesthetic sense is also an aid to communication, particularly in oral communication. This communication is not only shown in oral presentations but also in, for example, television. There are one or two well known specialists on television who communicate largely through their overwhelming enthusiasm. Why shouldn't students use the medium of television in order to see their own ability in communicating with others — both specialists and non-specialists, each with their own requirements?

Oral communication can be more formal — the presenting of a case. Again the rigours of debate, committee constraints, and specialist and non-specialist audiences are open for students to tackle. The case may include costing and environmental considerations for many technological developments, costing and political considerations for many social developments. The sense of audience is more obvious in some disciplines such as drama and less so in others such as the sciences and mathematics, but oral comunication is an important part of any course.

Written communication is incorporated as an axiom in many courses, but written communication for whom and for what purpose? A written case presented to a committee needs to be well argued and succinct, that to a professional body well referenced and scrupulously correct. How important is the technique of communication compared with the detailed regurgitation of facts or figures? Can simulated exercises be incorporated which may relate to oral communication?

Management of communication is another aspect of the communication with customers and clients (including advertising), with both manual and non-manual workers. Students who are on a sandwich type of course are in a better position to practise these elements than those on a full time course, for whom the practice may have to be through simulation and role playing. Are, then, our present assessment procedures too heavily biased on specialist-to-specialist communication with its associated rigour, at the expense of other forms of communication?

Developing a Philosophy of Life

Education should generate in students some sense of 'Who am I?' and 'Why am I here?' What is their role or purpose in life? What are the relative values of money and security in a job? What are the merits of a capitalist and a socialist society? There are many, many questions in this category. how can all this be fitted in when so much basic work has to be completed? The counter question is: 'What is the purpose of the education?' Is a scientist to be put in a position where he is unable to involve himself in discussions on the ethical, moral and political problems associated with scientific discoveries? Could it be that some of the problems in a technological society are related to the heavy bias to non-science disciplines in politics and the civil service and to the unwillingness of scientists to contribute to moral and ethical discussions?

These are problems of education and the purpose of education (Whitehead, 1932).

Developing Psychomotor Techniques

Psychomotor techniques are not only associated with crafts. Writing, reading, speaking, listening are all psychomotor activities. It may not be realistic to separate these developments from others, except that for most disciplines (other than perhaps language education, crafts and artistic subjects) little attention is paid to developing these attributes. However the use of the spoken word is partly a psychomotor skill. It is little use for a committee member or a presenter of a learned paper to speak in such a way that he cannot be heard. It is right to expect an educated person to be able to speak in public.

Faster reading techniques have been developed. However, sheer speed is insufficient unless supported by adequate comprehension. If the purpose of education is to enable students to learn to learn, then reading and comprehension of reading are key elements where improved efficiency can occur. It may be that keyboard dexterity (be it on a typewriter, a piano or a computer) is also of importance to most of us in our working life. Can useful and important activities such as these be omitted in order to cram in more facts and knowledge?

Aims and Objectives

Whilst it is important for long-term educational purposes to be as general as possible, there may be a case for a more rigorous specification in the short term. The area we are considering is a minefield of terminology: aims, goals, general objectives, specific objectives, behavioural objectives, process objectives, enabling objectives — not to mention purposes!

The general educational purposes are usually called *aims* and are attempts to answer 'What is education?'. The purposes that have been outlined so far in this chapter could be considered as elaborations of the aims:

(1) learning to learn;
(2) problem-solving techniques;
(3) communication techniques;
(4) developing a philosophy of life;

The normal discipline-based content could come under three of these purposes:

(1) learning to learn;
(2) problem solving techniques;
(3) communication techniques.

The conceptual framework of the discipline is an aid to learning. It enables the learner to relate detailed information to a structure; it is rather like a patterned note in its effect. The conceptual framework may enable some problem-solving and will certainly assist in communication with other specialists.

For the organisation of a course (or a curriculum) decisions are necessary on its purposes in general terms. These general purposes are used as a basis for the specific purposes of an individual course. A detailed specification for the previous two purposes might read 'distinguish between an aim and a purpose'. The Business Education Council (BEC) and the Technician Education Council (TEC) both use aims, general objectives and learning objectives in their course specifications. These specifications are the basis for the assessment procedures. There is now almost a tradition of words to use and not to use for specifying purposes or objectives. Some examples are shown below:

Words to Use	*Words Not to Use*
recognise	learn about
discriminate	appreciate
identify	discuss
list	know about
solve	think
find	understand
select	
estimate	
design	
assess	
interpret	
interact	
develop	
organise	
liaise	
integrate	

The verbs in the 'words to use' list are more specific, action-oriented and measurable. Herein lies one of the problems of detailed specification. The next step is to accept only detailed specification which can be measured. This may be perfectly acceptable in training and service courses and possibly in lower levels of learning, but becomes increasingly difficult in higher problem solving and in changes in attitude. It is helpful to the individual lecturer to have a clear idea of the purpose of individual sessions and of groups of sessions with students. Many students find it helpful to have the purpose made clear to them prior to the session. It is equally clear that for some learning sessions the learning purpose may be better clarified in a short de-briefing session afterwards.

Care must be taken to ensure that the purposes are not entirely content-oriented because experience shows that the purposes then become more trivial and related to lower levels of learning. This type of learning can be less satisfying to many learners. In a less structured learning situation another method is to get students to specify their own learning requirements. These requirements can be modified into purposes which are agreed between student and lecturer forming a contract for learning. Whichever system is used there seems to be little merit in keeping the purposes secret. The assessment should also be clearly related to purposes. For specific purposes defined boundaries are sometimes included, for example:

> *Classify* the list provided into three groups, *listing* each item under the heading defining the group. The classification to be completed with *not more than two errors within 15 minutes*.

The action verbs are 'classify' and 'listing'. The performance expected is 'not more than two errors' and the conditions are 'within 15 minutes'. This specification makes very clear the outcome of performance by the learner as an end point.

On service courses and basic courses another method of showing students the requirements is, at the beginning of the course, to give them a list of 20-40 questions that they would be expected to answer. The questions used in the end-of-course assessment would include questions like those given, but with variations in the basis of the question not the style of the question. For example in physics the question given at the beginning of the course may say:

> Uranium 235 is an isotope of uranium. What is meant by an isotope? How many neutrons and protons are there in Uranium

235? Show the first four elements in the decay series with their atomic number, atomic mass and the emissions.

The actual question may read:

Plutonium 240 is an isotope of plutonium. Wht is meant by an isotope? How many neutrons and protons are there in Plutonium 240? Show the first four elements in the decay series with the atomic number, the atomic mass and the emissions.

The student should be given a clear indication of which series are included and which are not.

In English the question at the beginning of the course may say:

In Macbeth compare the characters of Banquo and MacDuff. How do the characters portrayed by Shakespeare relate to the historical context of Shakespeare?

The actual question may be:

In Macbeth compare the characters of Macbeth and Duncan. How do these characters portrayed by Shakespeare relate to the historical context of Shakespeare?

Again the range of comparisons expected needs to be made clear.

This type of course specification has two effects; an expectation of high performance from all course members and a severe restriction on the range of possible variations from the specified learning. The specification may be acceptable for service and basic courses which serve as tools for later learning, but there is little evidence of use with final year degree courses. A simplified version has been used in most Open University courses (see any Open University text).

Conflict of Roles: Teacher v. Examiner

Often in further and higher education the examining is carried out by the person who did the teaching. There is a conflict between these roles. This conflict may not be apparent to all students. For those students who have previous experience of examinations set by external bodies the role of the teacher was essentially with the learner and against the examiner. The lecturer as teacher needs to withhold certain information in order to function in his role as examiner.

However, evidence collected in a study at Edinburgh University (Miller and Parlett, 1974) suggests that many students are able to derive probable examination questions merely by attending the course. The situation suggested at the end of the previous section does partially resolve the dilemma because the cards are clearly on the table, there is no secrecy nor any tricks involved. Another attempt to overcome the problem involves the use of continuous assessment, but that provides different conflicts which will be elaborated in the next chapter.

6 ASSESSMENT OF LEARNING

Assessment as Key Learning Materials

In most levels of continuing and higher education assessment plays a key role, but how and why? From a student's point of view the assessment procedures used (tests, examinations, essays) are the clearest indication of outcome. Even in a project the assessment may well act as the main initial motivation for many students. All assessment procedures (if well organised and managed) have enormous potential to aid learning. Assessment can be organised as a co-operative venture between students and lecturers or even between students and students, rather than a battle ground.

Try writing a list of all the possible purposes of assessment. If you can persuade some colleagues to do the same all the better — you can compare lists afterwards, first looking for differences and then trying to draw up some consensus list. See if you can divide the purposes into four or five different groups. After completion see how your classification compares with the one I have given in the last section of the chapter.

In this chapter we shall look at some particular types of assessment: tests, examinations, assignments, continuous assessment and projects. This is probably the range of types most commonly used by lecturers. The types will be considered for their use in helping students to learn and for helping the lecturer to identify individual student and group problems. The preparation of assessment procedures, the associated follow-up and feedback to students are key areas in the management and organisation of learning. What can a lecturer be expected to undertake within his normal duties? Do the marks allocated in assessments have any real meaning? A simple approach to assessment looks at two viewpoints, (a) assessment of the student, and (b) assessment of the course (usually called evaluation). Assessment of what, by whom and for whom?

Tests

The term 'tests' will be used to mean assessments which are not incorporated in marks leading to a qualification or classification. In particular it will be used for assessments done under specified conditions (for example, time limits and supervision).

The form of these tests can vary from short answer questions to open-ended essays or problem-solving. The tests are aimed at giving information to the student and/or the lecturer about problems that have occurred or are occurring in learning. There is no reason why the test has to be marked on the basis of answers or end point — with adequate supervision it can be marked on process.

Let us consider fairly typical end point type tests first of all. For example, multiple choice questions require students to select an answer from a series of options, the most usual number of which is four. This type is most suitable for testing knowledge, conceptual frameworks and simple applications of knowledge and concepts. The design of questions is similar regardless of whether they are used for feedback to students on their success in learning or for examination purposes (Rowntree, 1977). The question is made up from various elements; for example:

Elements in a Multiple Choice Question	*Name of Elements*
Osmosis is the process by which:	STEM
(a) food is made from light	DISTRACTOR
(c) molecules pass through a selective membrane	CORRECT OPTIONS or KEY
(d) molecules create new plants	DISTRACTOR

An example of one type of multiple choice question is shown above. The most effective way of selecting distractors is by use of a short answer question (in this case, 'What process is meant by osmosis?'). From the short answer question the most common student misconceptions can be derived. These misconceptions form the distractors for a multiple choice question for the following year. Having collected together a series of questions a number of management decisions are necessary such as:

1. How are the questions to be set? (using overhead projector transparencies, printed sheets, etc.
2. How are the questions to be answered? Are the answers to be processed by computer, and does the computer unit have special answer cards? Are students to ring, underline, tick an answer, a number, or a letter?
3. What information is required afterwards by the students, the lecturer, anyone else?
4. How is data on the performance of the questions year by year to be collected?

5. What action is expected from students and the lecturer on incorrect answers?

These sort of questions will be looked at in more detail in Chapter 9.

Let us consider some relevant points in relation to the use of such questions (or items) for diagnosis of learning problems. First of all it is not possible to test all possible learning combinations or knowledge. Since only a sample can be tested, the conclusions to be drawn on the basis of the test are limited. As the testing is for diagnostic purposes, totals have little meaning. Whether the student gets 68 per cent or 85 per cent does not diagnose problems. It is the details of the 32 per cent and 15 per cent which the student got wrong that diagnose problems. The actual questions that were wrong and in what way they were wrong is the key information. From the student's point of view the incorrect answers, the correct answer and the associated question are the important elements. It has been known for a fairly sophisticated system to be set up with question sheets, answer sheets for computer use, computer print-outs of individual student information as suggested — the student receiving his wrong answers and the key but no longer having access to the question. Obviously students not having access to the question defeats the whole object of the exercise.

The student, having found his answers wrong, is now expected to find out why and, if he does not understand, to ask. Unless the purpose of the test and the answers are made clear to student and to lecturers the test can be a massive waste of time. The test should be used to highlight problems. The lecturer should ask the student how he derived the wrong answer — only in this way is any attempt made to get at the process of the learning. The main criticism of much testing of the kind described is that there is an assumption that the correct answer indicates a correct process. The lecturer's work has not yet finished. He should notice which questions have been answered incorrectly by many students. If many students are getting answers wrong there are at least two main possibilities — a poor question or problems in learning — and both need investigation. Where problems in learning are occurring, it is necessary to go back to the students and in a co-operative venture endeavour to find the problems; next year, because the lecturer knows the students' likely problems, the new students' performance would perhaps improve more rapidly.

The multiple choice question has been used as an example in the account above. All the steps included in the sequence above apply equally well to all other forms of testing, literature searches, problem-solving, practical exercises, etc. In each the feedback to the students and the lecturer and the co-operative attempt to overcome learning problems are the primary purpose.

The more interaction it is possible to have with students *whilst they are carrying out the test*, the more information is available on the process of learning. Syndicates of learners may well be able to take over the role of diagnostic testing, especially if they know that they will get co-operation from the lecturer when learning problems arise which they cannot solve. If we are trying to help students to learn how to learn then the more they an be weaned into helping themselves the more successful we will have been. Here tests have not been considered for classification or qualification purposes. Only very occasionally is there any possibility of the test serving both purposes. When mastery of a technique is being tested (that is on a pass/fail basis), such as in medical diagnosis testing, dexterity skills, etc., then a dual role may be possible.

Examinations

The primary purpose of examinations is to produce a distribution of marks from which we can either select the best students required on a competitive basis or classify students on the basis of their performances in a variety of examinations. There is little doubt that these examinations may be based on the courses provided, but they are not absolute measures in any way. Why are we sometimes so dishonest about the purposes of examinations? Most students are not deceived. The rules of the game may not have been clearly laid down, nevertheless there are rules. When the rules are changed in any way it is only fair to students to make the changes explicit.

Examinations are educational materials. They are educational materials which take time to produce and the ensuing student materials take a considerable time to mark. For over forty year examinations have been known to suffer from appalling inaccuracies and inconsistencies in marking, in setting and in interpretation (Hartog and Rhodes, 1935), but at least we can ask on what basis we are trying to compare students. Many of us are familiar with the six or even twelve three-hour examinations in finals for degrees. Each examination is based on a different content area, but often requires the same abilities — at worst regurgitation of notes from the last three years, occasionally at best a unique, inspired original piece of written work or solution. Unfortunately in examination papers both types of question appear in the same paper as alternatives. The majority of students will play safe, learn all their notes and attempt the questions requiring mainly rote learning — they feel that it is the only safe and sensible way to work unless one is a genius.

Surely if a comparison is required, a global comparison is of dubious value. If there is to be such a comparison should not higher level problem-solving be more important than the rote learning? Of course certain base levels of knowledge are necessary; for end point classification purposes multiple choice type questions (or variations such as assertion — reason, matching, geomatrix) may be more efficient than essays for testing knowledge — especially if no further feedback is going to be given to the students. For normal examination purposes the questions need selecting because the questions are required to produce a distribution of marks rather than just sampling the course. Questions must contribute to the discrimination between students. Two indices commonly used are:

(1) *Facility* which is the proportion of students getting the question correct (there are variations in this calculation).
(2) *Discrimination* which is a comparison between the performance of students near the top and those near the bottom.

A question giving a good characteristic would expect to have about half the students getting the question correct and many more students near the top (on total) getting it correct than those near the bottom. (For detailed calculations see the literature on assessment.) Strictly this type of procedure should be applied to all types of questions for classification purposes. Those which do not have the correct characteristics should be rejected. Another series of questions might look at descriptive repetitive work, a further series at practical ability, another at solving provided problems, and yet another at generating problems. In this way a profile of the students' abilities can be drawn up rather than testing only memory of content.

By examinations we do not necessarily mean three hours of sitting in a silent examination hall. Examinations can be conducted in a laboratory, they can be literature searches, projects of dissertations, or they can be carried out by interview. Today there is no limit to the range of interpretations of examinations. However all are aimed at producing a range of marks to allow for classification. Unless a good range of marks occurs for each examination there will be close bunching when adding all the marks up, making classification more difficult. To aid classification it is essential that each examination and each question should use as wide a range of the available marks as possible. The preparation of a mark scheme is an essential piece of administration for any lecturer. The following questions need to be asked:

1. What is expected in the answer to a particular question?
2. How are the students likely to answer this question?
3. What group or range of marks will be allocated for different types of response?

These decisions can be made to produce a distribution of marks.

The numbers themselves have little meaning. The difference between 2 and 3 is not the same as that between 12 and 13 nor as that between 19 and 20 (especially for a question marked out of 20). There is no proper zero to the scale. The numbers which are given are barely suitable for the application of multiplication and division (Siegel, 1956). The errors in marking are going to be anything from about 2 per cent upwards, so that arguments over whether an average of 59 per cent is definitely a lower second (supposing the upper second to be over 60 per cent) are meaningless. All students around a borderline should be considered very carefully. The use of numbers alone to make the discrimination is suspect because of the error in those numbers.

There is evidence that employers are becoming increasingly aware of the doubtful classification barriers and are paying more attention to references than degrees (Cox and Collins, 1975). Perhaps the idea of a profile of grades may be a useful way forward (Klug, 1977, Rowntree, 1977). Whatever the system, the preparation of questions and mark schemes is of great importance.

Assignments

Assignments differ from tests because there is no time constraint. Students are usually allowed to complete the assignment in their own time and without supervision; thus there is more opportunity for co-operative working. The assignments may or may not be rigorously marked by the lecturer. (Why is co-operative working sometimes considered to be 'cheating'?) Assignments are much more obviously aimed at promoting learning than are tests or examinations. There is less pressure on the student to perform, although inevitably many students may wish to impress their lecturers on any piece of work. The need to perform will depend largely on the relationship between the lecturer and the student. Of all the assessment methods possibly assignments have the most potential for a co-operative learning venture. Some simple case studies will be considered to illustrate the potential of these educational materials.

Case Study 1

Students carrying out a laboratory course were required to write up their reports each week. The reports were collected and marked. The marking consisted of a tick and a brief comment, and then the report was returned. Students were bewildered. 'I honestly haven't a clue whether (the) report is used initially to see how we are doing, how we write things, or whether it is used for a formal mark or something. I would be interested in finding out.' It is clear that these assignments were of doubtful value. Why are students expected to write a report for every single experiment? If it is for the routine of report writing, is the repetition for two or three different laboratory courses over three years really necessary? If it is to interpret readings and data, why is the descriptive part necessary? Could the reports be considered as a separate exercise?

Case Study 2

In another laboratory course the students were provided with a work book with all the experiments in it. Each experiment had a work-sheet. Students were expected to answer some questions before proceeding to the laboratory work; these were checked soon after their arrival. In order to answer the questions the students had to read textbooks or even search in study packs or other information in the library. The actual time for the laboratory was considerably reduced (from 3 hours to 2 hours). Students were required to provide answers to specific questions on the work-sheet and explanations of their answers. The report writing was a separate exercise. Each student wrote two reports — one as a trial run, corrected and altered with the tutor's advice; the second was submitted for a mark, and again alternations were agreed, giving a second mark.

Case Study 3

A course in the social sciences was based on study p;acks and work-sheets. Each work-sheet had a general title and a more specific goal. A brief summary of the area under discussion was incorporated. Reference was made to text(s) and/or paper(s) in a study pack. Students had to prepare material (a) for the next seminar in which they were expected to contribute; (b) for an essay to be written on the topic. The essays were used for two purposes, feedback and examination.

Case Study 4

Another course used a study pack series on the role of behaviour in groups as a basis for the group activity. Each week not only were the students expected to read the material in the study pack, of which there were multiple copies, but also to participate in the group according to an agreed framework. Details of this method are incorporated in an excellent little booklet by Hill (1977).

Examples have already been cited of the engineers who watched a videotape in the library, took readings, made deductions and then went back to the library to compare their data with that of manufacturers and research workers before returning for a discussion with their tutor.

Assignments are a clear basis for encouraging students to learn for themselves (see Case Studies 2, 3, and 4). The learning process is active and many students are very much more enthusiastic, especially if it is clear in the short term where they are going. Have you tried driving or walking to a place whose name you are uncertain of, without the aid of a map? Assignments are important pieces of design and preparation work; through them a lecturer is encouraging students to learn to learn.

Continuous Assessment

This type of assessment has become more acceptable in recent years, partly because of student pressure to reduce the examination load. Although continuous assessment used in place of examinations may reduce the problems of examination nerves for some students, nevertheless it has added a considerable burden for others. The continual requirement to submit essays for marking, knowing that the marks are cumulative, is a heavy, nervous load for some students. Thus continuous assessment does not produce a reduction in student workload, but a spread which ensures more regular work from students. The problems of plagiarism are obviously present but are different from the usual interpretation of cheating in examinations (Cox and Collins, 1975). It is worth emphasising that 'continuous' is a misnomer. 'Intermittent assessment' would be more correct. There are few examples of continuous assessment, unless selection processes for pilots and managers are included; in these cases one's entire behaviour during the day is observed — and possibly during the night too!

All the assessment procedures outlined in the previous two sections along with the more conventional examinations can be placed under the heading of 'continuous assessment'. Lecturers and students often have the misconception that this type of assessment can satisfactorily perform two diverse roles; those of classification and of feedback. As soon as a student carries out an assignment in his own time the lecturer expects a higher minimum standard compared with an examination. The student also expects much more from it — so the student will give a better assignment, with a resulting tendency to raise the lower marks. At the same time the lecturer has a considerably higher expectation for the possible level of assignment that the student could attain. The first effect of continous assessment is usually that marks lie in a narrow middle band quite unsuitable for discrimination purposes.

Continuous assessment, which at first sight appeared to offer so much, re-emphasises the conflict of roles of the lecturer as teacher and as examiner. The conflict arises partly from the way in which assessment, like examination, sometimes fails to simulate real life. All forms of examination and assessment are a simulation, a game with rules (Miller and Parlett, 1974). Unfortunately in the examination the simulation element has been reduced to meet the needs of classification.

How can assessment be more realistic as a reflection of real life? Is it possible to allow groups of students, or syndicates, to provide work for assessment and examination?

Projects

Projects, dissertations and creativity have been mentioned in previous chapters. The idea of a higher level of learning and performance has already been discussed. The work is not always carried out individually; there are examples of groups working together on projects. The assessment of projects for classification purposes is usually carried out individually even though the project was worked through by a group.

Methods for the assessment of projects have been well documented (Adderley, 1975, Dowdeswell and Harris, 1978, Black, 1975). The problem is similar to that raised in the previous section; whether the project is a learning experience or an assessment procedure, and whether assessment based on the work during the project conflicts with the role of helping the learner. A further question arises as to whether an assessment based purely on the report is a fair reflection of the work during the project. Another problem is particularly associated with the assessment of projects. The supervisor gives considerable assistance to the student. Is the assessment an assessment of the student or of the supervisor? This problem really has two parts; (a) is it an assessment of the success of the supervisor to help the student, or (b) is it an assessment of how much work the supervisor has done towards the project? These problems highlight the need for a clarification of the purposes of the assessment.

Classification of Assessment

One classification suggests four ways of looking at assessment of students (Harris, 1975) and two ways of looking at assessment of courses, as shown below:

Students	*Courses*
comparative	formative
predictive	summative
diagnostic	
absolute	

Comparative assessment (sometimes called discriminative assessment) is used where it is required to discriminate between the performances of different students. This is the type of assessment used in the General Certificate of Education and in degree classifications. In spite of arguments that the assessment is based on the course and on the syllabus, nevertheless the intention is to classify students (Klug, 1977; Rowntree, 1977). The statistical techniques available are well advanced and are based on an assumption of a normal distribution.

Normal distribution

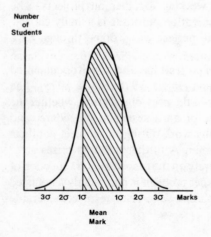

About 68 per cent of the students will be in the shaded area under the curve (the typical upper 2nd/lower 2nd group): σ represents the standard deviation which is computed by (a) calculating the difference (deviation) from the mean for each individual mark; (b) squaring that difference (deviation); (c) adding these squares; (d) dividing by the total number of marks; and (e) square rooting the final figure.

For much work on a comparative basis there is a deliberate attempt to produce this distribution even by adjusting marks by calculation to this distribution. Questions are often devised with four parts (a) a simple rote learning (e.g. a definition) that most students can answer; (b) a descriptive part which a large proportion can answer; (c) a problem or calculation which a smaller proportion can answer; and (d) a sting in the tail which few can answer. If the designer of such questions has judged well in relation to the target population, these will produce a normal distribution. Where choice is allowed in an examination it becomes important to ensure that *each* question has similar characteristics.

Predictive assessment is used in order to predict future performance. This type of assessment is sometimes used in continuing or higher education for decision on future courses (e.g. honours or pass degree). Aptitude tests and tests of manual dexterity may come into this category. There is a tendency to use 'O' levels, 'A' levels, degrees and other similar assessments as predictive of future success. The success of these examinations as predictors is associated with their comparative nature, not their design. In most cases these assessments are comparative assessments based on past work (i.e. looking backwards).

Diagnostic assessment is aimed at giving the student and the lecturer information on the student's progress at that point in time. From the information, which should be fed back to the student as soon as possible, the student can decide on or be advised about remedial work to improve his performance. It cannot be emphasised too much that the purpose is to give information on progress and not to classify students. One of the major problems with continuous assessment is a conflict between diagnostic and comparative assessment. Totals of scores are often superfluous in diagnostic testing. The information required is not an answer to the question 'What mark did the learner get?' but 'What problems is the learner having?'. This information is hidden in the totals, as outlined earlier.

Diagnostic testing is often associated with multiple choice questions and other similar types of tests. These types of tests will generally be used for assessing lower levels of learning. The questions are not easy to design but the marking is easy and can be associated with computer handling for ease of processing. Another simple form consists of bringing into a class an overhead projector transparency bearing six key words, phrases or quotes that relate to, say, a term's work. For each word the students are asked to write for about one minute. This is carried out without previous warning and gives good feedback on student problems both to lecturers and students if the answers are studied in class. This can then be followed immediately with another similar transparency relating to the next term's work in order to focus students' attention on work that is to come.

Absolute assessment is less common in higher education than continuing or further education. For certain professions and jobs it is essential that a certain minimum level of competence should be demonstrated. Tests are devised to assess this competence on a pass or fail basis (e.g. number of words typed in a minute with specified maximum errors from a document provided; accurate mixing of medicines and drugs in solid or liquid form). An absolute assessment can only be based on a small sample of a domain of available tasks. This type of assessment lends itself to practical, mathematical and linguistic studies. In absolute assessment if marks are allocated, there is usually an expectancy of quite high marks, with a skewed distribution.

Skewed distribution

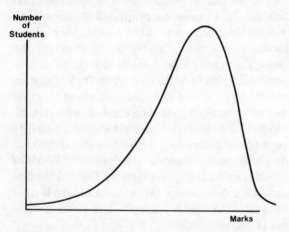

In the educational literature there are various classifications given to *course assessment*. However in the context of the individual lecturer in relation to his own course many of these are superfluous.

For administrators, or senior staff with a more global view, some of the appropriate literature is elaborated in the back of this book.

The individual lecturer may well wish to know whether his course or lecture is effective. Each individual may have a different perception of the word 'effective'; it could be one or more of the following:

(1) a good personal performance — voice, presentation;
(2) students learning a lot of factual data;
(3) students getting a good set of notes;
(4) students enjoying the lecture/course;
(5) students going on and carrying out follow-up work with or without further encouragement — solving problems, reading references, asking questions;
(6) students achieving goals laid down for the lecture/course;
(7) students being very interested or excited about the lecture/course.

No doubt further statements could be added. You may like to try your own list.

Using the list above as a guideline, let us look at what methods can be used. Possible sources of information are:

(1) academic colleagues;
(2) students;
(3) examination answers;
(4) tests;
(5) questionnaires;
(6) free responses;
(7) video or audio recordings of the lecture/course;
(8) one's own opinions;
(9) observation.

If the collection of information is systematic the details of modifications to the course or lecture can be worked out with more certainty. A more detailed look at all these mthods will be considered in Chapter 11.

By developing the methods of student assessment it is clear that we can get information on the effectiveness of learning from diagnostic tests and answers to examination questions. From diagnostic tests we are interested in common problems across groups of students (for example the number of students getting a question wrong on a multiple choice question *and* which wrong answer they chose or even how many omitted the question). From examination questions we can find out how many students avoided the question (does this tally with previous years?), and what parts of the question were poorly answered by many or most students.

Using this information we now have a clue to learning problems; what misconceptions arose, and what did students avoid (and so presumably found difficult)?

The first step is to take a careful look at the examination or test item. How do other colleagues or students interpret it? Is there any ambiguity? Only if it is clear that the problem does not lie here, will it be sensible to progress to modifying the learning situation. This is a joint problem between the lecturers and the students — why not try and solve it jointly?

7 MODES OF LEARNING

Student as Learner

Modes of learning include lectures, small group work, laboratory work and individual work. An important part of these modes is the role of the lecturer and the learner. The most common arrangement of teaching is by use of the lecture, with the lecturer as active participant and the learners as passive receptors. Subordinate activities consist of small groups or laboratory work. Individual work is assumed to be almost exclusively the responsibility of the learner. The advantage of the lecture is that the lecturer can argue forcefully that *he* has covered all the work, the rest is up to the student. This provides considerable security for the lecturer and at first sight security for the learner. Working from the individual as learner provides considerable insecurity for the lecturer because he feels that he has no control on what is happening; he can no longer say 'I have covered that'. The onus for learning is placed squarely on the student's shoulders. For many this will be an alien experience compared with school, where the teachers provided a mechanism to enable the learner to pass the examinations — a sort of spoon feeding. How can students be weaned from this approach?

It cannot be emphasised too often that the person who actually has to do the learning is the student. The most likely success for heavily teacher-centred modes is when the examinations or assessments test repetition of factual material. A student need not raise his sights above rote learning, but this is merely a narrow interpretation of learning, not compatible with education, and hardly ever with training.

Individual Learning Methods

Let us consider some of the principles involved in individual learning methods. A variety of descriptions are used for different aspects of individual learning. Self instruction usually refers to a formal organised or structured sequence of learning material (for example programmed learning or synchronised tape/slide sequences). These structured sequences may or may not incorporate assessments. At the othr end of the spectrum is independent learning, where 'independent' should suggest that the decisions on strategy, sequence, content, and assessment are made by the learner independently. To incorporate all

73

these elements of independence is unusual. If only one element is incorporated as independent, the larger part of the learning is organised by the lecturer; so is it really independent learning or is it self *instruction*? Some lecturers interpret independent learning as meaning that they are not present, yet some self instructional materials are even more lecturer-dependent than lectures.

The Lecture

It is quite possible within a lecture for the learner to develop his own materials based on the presentation. It has already been shown that patterned notes are idiosyncratic to the individual learner. These notes give a relationship between the learner's experience and what is to be learned.

The Book

One of the earliest individual learning methods does not depend on electricity, can be taken anywhere and has easy access to any part of it — the book. The message that is received from this book will be dependent on factors like past experience and whether ideas are in agreement or in conflict with the material. Some people will simply read the book, some will make notes, some will also read from the books given in the annotated bibliography, some will discuss with colleagues — each learner reacting as an individual. The important element is probably why one got hold of the book in the first place — was there a particular problem or need — often the best motivator.

Group Discussion

A group involved in a discussion again allows for individual learning. Some participants will be active and wish to express their ideas for criticism, some will express their ideas and be dogmatic or defensive, some will merely criticise and yet others will be apparently passive. Interaction with other human beings through language is one clear criterion which separates us from the rest of the animal kingdom. Language is the medium of interaction, whether it is oral, symbolic or pictorial. The spoken word is the means by which we are often required to convince the manager, the worker or the customer. Experience in determining reactions to our methods of verbal communication occur through discourse. The group discussion can enable us to learn about the interaction as well as learning about the views of others. However whether the group is formed as a seminar, tutorial, a leaderless group or a syndicate the needs of each individual learner are important.

Television and Audio

Individual learning is the basis for Open University courses and correspondence courses such as those organised by the National Extension College. The television productions of the Open University are worth experiencing to see a means of encouraging students to maintain a schedule and for giving an overall view of a topic to be studied in depth by the student; they also use radio broadcasts in many courses, more particularly those in the Arts and Social Sciences.

In an insitution where students regularly attend lectures there is an imposed schedule. However the availability of recorded material in television and in audio format is a means of presenting materials and ideas which do not fit into normal teaching. For individual study, television has a very powerful role; where the student views his own performance systematically, either a real life situation or a simulation. The range of use of this style of learning varies from training teachers (often associated with a technique called microteaching), social workers, lawyers and doctors, to helping sportsmen and ballet dancers perfect their techniques. In each case a recording is made of the performance of the learner or their interaction with others. The use of check lists or guided questions enables the learner to begin to evaluate his own performance.

Work-Sheets

A less sophisticated means of requiring students to work on their own is by using work-sheets. The work-sheet can be a laboratory work-sheet or a work-sheet which outlines other work to be carried out. A work-sheet can vary from being very open ended to being very prescriptive. By changing the format of work-sheets gradually from prescriptive to open ended it is possible to wean students from their dependence on the lecturer. Work-sheets can be used in association with virtually any mode or media, because they require less detailed preparation than some formalised methods of self-instruction and are more easily adapted year by year.

A prescriptive work-sheet may have several section, for example:

(1) goals or objectives to be met;
(2) a *brief* outline of the topic;
(3) a few references (by book, chapter or actual paper);
(4) an annotated bibliography of the references;
(5) an assignment to be completed which meets the specified goals (it might be several problems or an essay).

The students have to carry out the work themselves, but within clearly delineated boundaries.

A less structured work-sheet may have a variation on those sections:

(1) a very general set of open questions;
(2) a brief introduction to the area;
(3) one or two leading references;
(4) a requirement for students to work out with the lecturer the goals for an assignment;
(5) an assignment to meet the students goals, an associated unspecified literature search and an expectation of a degree of originality.

In both cases the student is expected to do the work. Instead of the lecturer spending time in presenting facts, the student has to find them to form a base for the assignment, whereas the lecturer has to prepare carefully, organise the work-sheet and the associated reference material, and work through the assignments. The larger the group the more difficult this technique becomes.

The Keller Plan

The Keller plan is an attempt to deal with some of the management problems associated with a prescriptive work-sheet. Because of the limitations of time available to lecturers (more particularly associated with the less favourable staff/student ratios in the United States of America), the regular assessment and testing associated with individualised instruction (another variation on the jargon) is carried out by senior students. For example a first-year student may have as his 'proctor' a third-year student. The third-year student marks assessments (assignments or tests) and indicates problem areas and whether the first-year student is to progress to the next piece of work or re-cycle the present one. The system is organised and carried out in collaboration with the professor or lecturer. The third-year student gains credits for his tutoring role and/or payment (see page 78).

Programmed Learning

A more prescriptive approach uses programmed learning. Here all the learning materials need to be analysed carefully and selected in order to produce a sequence of learning prescribed by the lecturer. it is difficult to build into the programme requirements for the student to develop his own framework, because the basis of the design is that students are given immediate knowledge of their responses to questions — there are right or wrong answers. Whilst lending itself effectively to factual and skilled approaches it is not a method to be recommended for opening up new ideas or creativity.

Structural Communication

Another form of individualised instruction is called structural communication. Whereas the basis of programmed learning is a sequential development of parts, structural communication aims at the whole. The learning materials are nearer to the work-sheets outlined earlier in this section. The tests do not expect right and wrong answers. According to the group of statements selected from a table of statements, a dialogue or discussion is developed. The student's opinion is not brushed aside as being wrong, but discussed on the basis of the data provided. A similar testing procedure is used by the Open University for its computer-marked assignments (Hodgson, 1974; OU Student Handbook, section on computer-marked assignments). A review of the varieties of individualised learning are given in a paper by Goldschmid and Goldschmid (1974).

Learning with Other Learners

The idea of using other learners as a resource has been mentioned several times within this book. As any lecturer will know, there is no better way of learning about something than having to teach it. Why shouldn't the learners benefit from this experience? Using learners from later years to act as tutors or proctors to learners in their first year has already been discussed. Bearing in mind that work to date has been initiated by enthusiasts for the system, the available evidence shows:

(1) benefit to students;
(2) benefit to tutor;
(3) students who act as tutors not only gain in cognitive learning, but also have a more positive attitude towards their course and an improvement in self-esteem;
(4) students are more willing to attempt difficult tasks;
(5) students enjoy peer teaching;
(6) students have a wider range and depth of reading than equivalent students on conventional courses.

The performance of these learners on conventional examinations shows no great variation from other students. However the examinations do little to assess the elements listed above.

In the previous section the Keller plan (also called Personalised System of Instruction: PSI) was briefly introduced. It is one of several methods using students who are more advanced in their course. In many courses in universities in the United Kingdom young graduates (usually carrying out research) are used as demonstrators; in the United States graduate assistants are used. Arguments put forward *against* their use include (a) that these students are often having major problems in their research and may well have just got married, so the 'teaching' is not taken very seriously, and (b) that the undergraduate students often view them as part of the authority/lecturer group: 'I am afraid I do not know who is a demonstrator and who is a lecturer.' The advantage of using a student who is in a later undergraduate year in the same course is that he is still very much involved in learning, and can see the benefits of reinforcing some of his own background. Students who have been tutored by senior students are very willing and enthusiastic about taking on the role themselves at a later stage. The method becomes a co-operative venture rather than the chore perceived by graduate students.

If the system is initiated as soon as the new students arrive the more advanced students can also take on a simple counselling role too, involving advice on housing, transport and use of the library, leading later to note-taking, examinations and the curriculum. The older students in turn meet the lecturers and professors for discussion of problems on the course.

Obviously these 'unequal' learners acting as tutors are different from the syndicate learning proposed in earlier sections. The use of unequal learners in no way acts as a panacea for all problems. The whole course needs designing around this method. The students must not only see that it is a useful system in theory but also in fact. In order to operate as a system, appropriate strategies for learning materials, lectures, seminars and laboratories need to be adopted. A regular feedback session with the undergraduate tutors is essential. There may be conflict between the assessment procedures used at present, which encourage competitive learning, and those used in this system, which encourage co-operative learning. There is also a problem in allocating small rooms for the groups to meet.

The main suggestion so far in this book has related to learners of equal status as syndicates. The ideal size of these syndicates would appear to be not more than six students. The problem of arranging such groups is hazardous. There is evidence of problems occurring between different character traits, different sexes, role-taking capacity and so on. The advantage of pairs is that some of the problems may be easier to resolve. In addition students can be persuaded to alternate roles as tutor and learner. The encouragement of informal groups rather than delegated groups may have some advantages. What is quite clear is that some structure is necessary for the operation of a system using learning with other learners. The system appears to function best when used with other teaching and learning methods. The important decision relates to the relative merits seen for students developing responsibility for their own learning associated with co-operation and social interaction.

Other Modes

Only when a decision has been made on whether the basic learning is to be carried out by the individual and how much time is to be allocated for that mode, can the role of other modes of learning be considered. Strategies for the presentation in lecture form have been elaborated in detail by Bligh (1972) in his book *What's the Use of Lectures?* If learners are expected for the most part to carry out most of their work individually then what is the role of the large group? Is it a means of collecting together ideas or of presenting ideas? Is it a means of providing information or relating information to a conceptual framework, or even of relating to the outside world? The difficulties of participation by students in lectures has been outlined in this book and in others (Bligh, 1972; McLeish, 1968). Their origin was largely associated with the opportunity to 'sit at the feet of' an acknowledged thinker or expert! The principal advantage of the lecture is in terms of time, cost and convenience — it is possible to use only one lecturer's time and have a lot of students present. Unfortunately in many institutions this has not been seen as a means of providing the student with work to get on with in his own time, but as a means of filling the week with more lectures. We have to ask ourselves seriously how much help this provides to the learner? What evidence is there that it is effective as well as economic use of academic staff? (Dubin and Taveggia, 1968). Would more occasional meetings for students in smaller groups (using the same amount of staff time) be more effective? Would fewer meetings but in smaller groups be more effective? At present there is little research evidenced for deriving answers to these questions. What has been shown by the Open University is that students can attain good standards and work mainly on their own if a large effort is put into the production of learning materials. Is there a compromise somewhere in between?

There are other factors which may contribute. The proportion of mature students may increase quite rapidly in the future, and obviously their needs are different from those of younger students. Mature students are often worried by assessment but less worried by classification. Their motives for learning are much clearer and a student-centred approach may make much more sense for learners who are highly motivated.

In a lecture there is a need for a much clearer understanding between the lecturer and his students. This understanding will include the purposes of the experience, the expectations of the lecturer *and* the students, and regular exchanges of feedback both ways. Nor is it sufficient for this to be done by one lecturer on the course — each set of students is a *different* group with each lecturer. It is a need for *each* lecturer with *each* group. This means a careful preparation of the lecture course and associated groups to enable the interchange to take place. No longer is it sufficient for a lecturer to say 'I tell them what I think is necessary; if they don't understand — well that's up to them.' Only if the whole course has built into it syndicates or unequal learner groups can this sort of statement have any place.

Encouragement can be given to students in the early stages to develop an idiosyncratic note-taking system (see Chapter 2). It is important that study methods are carefully nurtured, not ignored. If students are clear about their own note-taking and the lecturer is consistent in his presentation (even if that consistency amount to a brief outline of the variation in presentations) the possibility of improved communication has been laid. Why not check students' notes from time to time to see how effective you have been? In addition let the students check your notes! (Their note format may well be very different from yours.)

8 MEDIA OF LEARNING

Media for Learning

What is meant by the word 'media'? What media are used for learning? There is a tendency to consider media as the mass media of television, radio and print. In a learning situation the human voice, gesticulations, hand-written notes, duplicated hand-outs, chalkboards, displays, specimens, models, overhead projectors, slide projectors, filmstrip projectors and 16 mm projectors are the more common media. Possible uses of media are:

(1) engaging the students' motivation;
(2) revision of work already covered;
(3) providing new learnig stimuli;
(4) activating students' responses;
(5) 'comment' on students' response (e.g. replay of a student's own performance such as language laboratory, or a video recording of a role-playing situation);
(6) manipulation of size, time, distance, attention and amount of information available.

What criteria can be used to judge the effectiveness of these media for learning? There are a range of criteria that can be considered. Some examples (not ranked in order of importance) are:

(1) cognitive learning (at a variety of levels);
(2) affective learning (at a variety of levels);
(3) psychomotor learning (at a variety of levels);
(4) entertainment value;
(5) interactive possibilities;
(6) freedom of choice in use by learner;
(7) cost;
(8) ease of use;
(9) ease of production/provision;
(10) specificity/generality;
(11) potential size of audience.

Let us consider one or two media in relation to these criteria.

Example 1

150 students are being given a lecture by a lecturer, using the chalkboard, hand-outs and the overhead projector. From the evidence available the lecture is as effective as almost any other method except programmed learning at lower levels of cognitive learning (criterion 1). The personality of the lecturer and his performance will determine its effectiveness both at these levels and in the lower levels of affective learning (criterion 2). However for higher levels of both domains it is a very inefficient method (Beard, 1972; Bligh, 1972). For psychomotor learning (criterion 3), the lecture has limitations unless carefully structured individual repetition is involved. It may be possible to have 150 students learning lower-level techniques such as typing (if 150 typewriters are available) but it is not a suitable method for higher psychomotor levels. As entertainment (criterion 4) the media being used would generally be rated low by students. Why should entertainment be considered as a criterion for learning? Learning is a serious business not fun — but why shouldn't learning be fun and enjoyable? Certainly the use of entertainment techniques may assist the level of attention, but if carried too far may also lead to distraction! The interactive possibilities (criterion 5) in the lecture are limited, but can be contrived by the deliberate use of buzz groups (small problems are given to which groups of four students are asked to devise solutions) (Bligh, 1972). There is no freedom of choice in use (criterion 6).

The cost (criterion 7) appears quite small. However not only is the same or a similar presentation given each year (with the cost of the lecturer's time) but also the original version will probably have taken 10 hours or more of preparation, with further time for modification each year. When compared with the preparation of simple self-instructional material the cost effectiveness will be marginal. For ease of use (criterion 8) a lecture is simple from students' point of view — or is it? What sort of notes should they take? How should the notes be organised? How does this lecture fit in with others? The ease of provision and production ranks high for the lecturer (criterion 9) — it is only a one-hour commitment, not the 50-100 hours that would be necessary for a more sophisticated technique. The preparation involves structuring and ordering the content, organising and preparing any hand-outs, overhead projector transparencies, the chalkboard layout and any other subsidiary aids. In relation to specificity/generality (criterion 10), a lecture can be placed almost anywhere along the spectrum, although it is normally used as the specific requirement for the particular students on that course at that time in their course; assumptions are made about their background knowledge, interest and expectations. The same presentation might well be suitable for an audience from 50 to 200 (criterion 11) but above or below that range it would be necessary to give a more informal presentation or a performance respectively.

What alternative media can be used and what changes in expectations, costs and effectiveness occur? The use of work-sheets and associated printed material would require more preparation, less contact time, more library resources, be as good if not better on potential interactive possibilities (especially with other students), give more freedom in choice of use and be able to provide for a wider range of audience. In addition the student would be expected to be more active.

Example 2

A group of 16 students are using a small television studio to record their performance as interviewers. Each pair is recorded, being observed by most of the rest of the group using a schedule or checklist. The previous pair are observing their own performance, playing back the videocassette recording in a small room (with the video recorder under their control), accompanied by two other students who were observers. The tutor watches most recordings, making notes for a de-briefing session and assisting the observation group, but going in with a pair on playback if a major problem has arisen. The amount of low-level cognitive learning (criterion 1) will be very limited whilst the motivation associated with the higher cognitive levels is high (criterion 2). There is inevitable entertainment value (criterion 4), albeit unsolicited on most occasions! The interaction potential (criterion 5) is enormous, both student to student and tutor to student. The freedom of choice of use (criterion 6) is partly in the hands of the students, particularly in the replay of their own performance. The cost (criterion 7) of this exercise is high in terms of equipment, space, technical staff, tutor's time — to be carried out effectively it will probably need the equivalent of a whole day. Provided the tutor has been systematic in his preparation, organisation and de-briefing the procedure is fairly easy to use (criterion 8) by students, although high on the use of nervous energy! The recordings and the procedure are highly specific (criterion 10) and would probably be of little use to others unless edited extracts were assembled. It would be difficult to cater for a much larger audience (criterion 11). In terms of cost effectiveness it is expensive, but what other method can be used with such a potentially large effect?

How much distortion is possible before learning media produce so much distress or annoyance to students that the learning is inhibited? Where is the boundary between what is acceptable and what is not acceptable? How does this boundary relate to costs of production? Whatever the media, including print, only limited evidence is at present available. The needs of learners are not the same as readers of popular novels or of television entertainment programmes. Both the popular novel and the television entertainment programme have a need to be attractive initially. The novel, presuming it is well written can be on poor paper and cheaply printed — once it has been bought the publisher has been successful. The television programme needs to maintain a standard of production, (a) to encourage the viewer to remain on that channel and (b) to prevent the viewer switching off. The learner is less difficult to catch in the first place, but does need some elements of motivation to maintain his attention. Whilst some of the techniques used in the production of a popular novel and an entertainment programme are helpful in learning materials, how many are essential?

For most learning situations in continuing, further and higher education, the purpose of any medium is to enable the student to learn. Provided that the materials follow the 'grammar' of the medium, the student will be able to learn from them (e.g. Davies, 1974). Highly professional materials help to motivate students, but the actual learning is more heavily dependent on content. Costs often rule out very professional productions in print or any other medium. Would the learners like extravagant professional presentations? What evidence exists to support the necessity? Only when a large production run is possible is a large investment in excellence of design feasible.

Very low levels of production seem to be acceptable for materials which are produced by the lecturer himself or where the motivation of students is very high. For highly motivated students the worst copies of typed or printed materials or of television replays seem to be acceptable. To students who are not motivated such productions would be treated as a joke and not worthy of consideration.

At the opposite extreme one of the problems of elaborate productions is that the purpose of the learning can be entirely lost. For example, students in an institution were required to use a computer terminal. The most elaborate, well designed (from a media point of view) television production was used. The students watched the production as a group and then went to use the terminal. Few were successful. After a trial with a synchronised tape slide production the same results occurred. It was only at this stage that some careful thought was given to what the purpose was. The student was not expected to remember everything by heart, but to be able to operate the terminal. A well designed booklet in colour with index tabs was attached to the terminal. The first few pages gave a brief introductory run. The remaining pages were an algorithmic presentation to enable users to overcome most problems that arose. The cheapest solution using the printed medium also provided the most effective learning for the purpose that was required.

Sometimes more elaborate techniques are cost effective. In the audio tutorial approach (Postlethwaite *et al.*, 1971) the student is provided with his own study materials and taped or written instructions. The study carrel used may include real objects or models, charts, displays, video, film, filmstrip, slides, actual experiments — any combination. The student works in his own time on an open-access basis within fixed hours. Although the design of the learning materials is elaborate, the utilisation of space and staff is greatly improved (Roach and Hammond, 1976) with good tutorial contact built into the course.

In an economics course an analysis was carried out based on answers to past examination questions. Two particular areas were followed in depth — questions on which students wrote poor answers and questions which were avoided. On analysis it was found that one of the main problems was mathematics. Because no extra time was made available for remedial mathematics, a series of short pieces of simple programmed learning were devised and tested. These pieces of programmed learning used economics problems associated with the mathematics. Since the introduction of the programmes, the pattern of answering examination questions has markedly changed, with mathematical problems becoming not only more popular but also answered at a level which was comparable with other questions. This is a good example of a hole-plugging and patching exercise carried out by one lecturer within the constraints of an organisation of curriculum over which he has very limited control. The programmed learning was used by students both for assignments and in class.

One of the problems of training consecutive interpreters is to convince them that there is no fixed format for taking notes; each interpreter has his own style of note-taking. A video recording was made of two professional interpreters, the emphasis in the picture being on the notes. Each interpreter was then shown using his notes for interpretation. Whilst the style and format of the notes were vastly different the duration and content of the interpretations were almost identical. It is not feasible to provide professional interpreters for every group of students to watch. The impact of a dynamic visual presentation is greater than handing out duplicated copies of the interpreters' notes. For cost effectiveness what would have been the impact of audio tapes of the original, the interpretation in association with the duplicated copies of the notes?

For most situations the development of learning materials is a long process. It is unusual for a large amount of time to be available to develop the materials. A systematic development of the parts to produce the whole learning sequence may take several years. As a result it is sensible to produce initial forms that can be fairly easily modified and updated. Nothing is more frustrating than a large expenditure of resources, energy and time in developing materials which immediately need modification. The larger the expenditure of resources, energy and time, the more permanent the end product. Do we really want such permanent end products in further and higher education?

If such high-quality end products are required, a joint development may be necessary with other institutions, or else available materials (e.g. broadcast or Open University television programmes, films from film libraries, texts) may be used with the idosyncracies of the local course built around these. It will be necessary to study and analyse these materials in order to decide how they will be used and how much of them will be used. Students can be good advisers in these decisions, after all they are learning from a very different base than us. What assumptions are made that are unrealistic for students? What facilities are available and accessible to students (e.g. television playback, copies of books)?

A range of media are listed in the table, although this list is by no means comprehensive. There is some pattern within the figure, but you may wish to re-arrange it to relate to the learning materials that you are likely to prepare. Some of the elements overlap (e.g. drama and television), some overlap with modes. Although attempts have been made to classify media and modes, these are of academic interest. What is more important is how do learners use these resources. Some students are analytical in their use of pictures, other are more holist (see Chapter 2). Some students learn better when presented with material in more than one format — so, for example, any of the normal audio visual presentations are most effective when supported by printed materials using extracts of the key visual material (e.g. a hand-out or booklet with the same pictures, diagrams in black and white instead of colour). Brief notes with the opportunity for students to fill in their own notes may be more effective than highly structured notes, although the evidence is inconclusive (Howe and Godfrey, 1977).

Library and Media

In a previous chapter a description was given of a group watching a television recording and then moving out into the library to look up available materials. Are media like television best viewed by individuals or groups? Certainly pairs of students with one or the other student assuming a tutor role using any form of self-instructional audio visual media seem to have advantages. Not only does the material they are using have to be less structured, but also the learning problems are more apparent to a peer acting as teacher. There seems to be little need to put a complete programme on television. Most students nowadays are familiar with a domestic or portable audio cassette recorder. The design of the controls on a video recorder have been made very similar. The recorder has a *stop* and a *rewind* control. If any part is not clear it can be viewed several times. The recording will often not be of broadcast standard, but from limited resources the student does not have that level of expectation. If the recording is associated with printed material and is indexed (for example by a digital clock superimposed in one corner of the picture) a very adaptable learning facility is available which each individual can use according to their needs.

Although film projectors for individual viewing are available, they are not common in libraries at present. The synchronised audio tape and 8 mm film (allowing moving and still frames to be used) has shown most potential, although the programming is more sophisticated than for most other formats.

Audio recording with booklets, 35 mm slides, filmstrip or more recently microfiche, lends itself to packages, and to self-instruction. There is evidence to suggest that associated printed materials (work-sheets, questions, problems) help students. In addition, working in pairs enables some resolution of problems in learning. The variety of formats have advantages and disadvantages but let us consider some of them in more detail.

Some media and their characteristics

	Individual	Group	Live	Recorded	Interactive
human voice and gesture (lecture, tutorial, drama)	✓	✓	✓		✓
manuscript notes, diagrams, etc.	✓			✓	
chalkboard, whiteboard, overhead projector, flipchart		✓	✓		
sound amplification	✓	✓	✓		
duplicated notes, work-sheets, bibliographies, references, pictures, photographs, diagrams, study packs, text books, programmed learning texts, journals	✓			✓	
specimens, working models, wall displays	✓	✓		✓	
audio tapes, disc recordings (aural)	✓	✓		✓	
language laboratories, audio tutorials	✓	✓		✓	✓
slides, filmstrips	✓	✓		✓	
synchronised sound and vision (still)	✓			✓	
moving vision with/without sound: FILM		✓		✓	
moving vision with sound: TELEVISION (local production or recording)	✓	✓	✓	✓	
feedback classroom		✓	✓		✓
electronic blackboard	✓	✓		✓	
correspondence course	✓			✓	?
telephone tutoring/videophone	✓	✓	✓		✓
electronic mail	✓			✓	✓
computer-managed learning	✓			✓	?
computer-assisted learning	✓	✓	✓	✓	✓
radio broadcasts	✓	✓	✓		
television broadcasts	✓	✓	?	✓	
PRESTEL/teletext	✓			✓	

Synchronised Audio and Still Picture

Slides with an associated magnetic recording disc have the advantage of easy replacement of individual slides, less attraction for the recording format to be removed for domestic use, but require special replay equipment. The microfiche associated with audio tape has a simple quick re-access to any of 60 frames on the microfiche and it recovers synchronisation for any stop or rewind, each frame being individually coded in the synchronisation. However, the format, whilst being European is not compatible with many microfiche formats used in the UK. For simpler microfiche machines it is probably easier to transfer to the format of the synchronised machine. The storage is less difficult for both these formats than audio tape synchronised with slides in the conventional way. Although there is a standard specification, many pulsing systems are incompatible.

Television Recordings

For videotape there are three basic formats: reel to reel, video-cassette and video-cartridge. On the reel to reel the machine must be threaded by hand. In a videocassette machine a mechanism collects the tape and threads the machine. In a video-cartridge machine the leader is of acetate which is automatically threaded on to the reel inside the machine. For library use the video-cartridge machine has the advantage that it must be rewound to extract it from the machine. This means that whenever a student collects or takes a video-cartridge he knows it will be at the beginning of the run. The video-cassette can be removed without rewinding, which can produce annoyance for the next user. The reel to reel machine, whilst having the inherent advantage of the video-cartridge machine for starting at the beginning, suffers from the disadvantage of student access to the mechanism and of incorrect threading. Most formats (even within video-cassettes) are incompatible with one another. For all library materials where rewinding is a problem it is worth ensuring that the last picture and the last sound instruction requests students to rewind the tape. In practice most users will respond.

Working in Groups

Students appear to enjoy using resources like videotape, synchronised audio and still pictures in groups (Harris and Kirkhope, 1974). If the equipment is in an open area of the library this will require multiple-channel earphones. In a separate relatively sound-proofed room the loudspeaker can be used.

Printed Materials and Microfiche

Printed materials (the book has been considered earlier) and microfiche (or microfilm versions) have a wide range of variations. Printed diagrams associated with audio tapes are cheaper and easier to use than some synchronised machines, but lack some of the impact of a projected medium. The principal advantage of this type of resource being in the library is the possibility of associating it with other work using books and journals. What evidence is available provides little information on the relative merits of locally produced and externally produced material. It is thought that talking heads are more acceptable if students know or can identify with the speaker. If professional advice is available it is worth seeking assistance in productions.

There is some evidence that students prefer to have work-sheets or printed material associated with the audio visual materials that are used in the library, preferably something that they can take away with them (Harris and Kirkhope, 1977).

When the quantity of materials grows, a cataloguing system becomes imperative. The catalogue can be based on the usual library classification system (e.g. Dewey) or on simplified systems (see for example Davies, W.J.K., 1978). not only is it helpful for the materials to be in the main catalogues but also in a local catalogue for the media resources on a disciplinary basis.

Assessment Associated with Media

Media can for example:

(1) engage the students' motivation;
(2) revise work already covered;
(3) provide new learning stimuli;
(4) activate students' responses;
(5) 'comment' on students' responses (e.g. a replay of a student's own performance such as language laboratory, or a video recording of a role-playing situation);
(6) manipulate size, time, distance, attention, and amount of information available.

Because of this diversity of possible uses it is clear that there are no simple answers on assessment using visual media. Some ingenious assessment procedures have however been used with visual media. For example, examinations of patients by doctors have been presented to trainee doctors. The trainee is required to speak a diagnosis into an audio recorder, stating what further information would be needed. The recording is marked and, where necessary, the trainee is required to explain in more detail the reasons for his decisions. Whilst this may be more impersonal than conventional examinations by trainee doctors, it is possible to have more control on the situation and to present the same case to several trainees simultaneously.

With synchronised audio tape and visual presentations, pauses can be built into the programme during which students are requested to recognise or diagnose pictorial information or even to answer multiple choice type of questions. The assessment is integated with the audio visual material and can be used for either comparative or diagnostic purposes. In addition the effectiveness of the learning materials can be determined from the students' responses. The methods can be used with groups or with individuals.

Learning and the Media

All media are effectively tools of learning. They are also tools of communication, the lecturer, and those who help him to produce the materials being in the role of communicator. Well produced materials release the lecturer for roles that a range of media cannot carry out. In particular human interaction allows an infinite variation in thought patterns. No book or machine can attain that degree of complexity.

As long ago as 1912, Thorndike wrote, 'A human being should not be wasted in doing what forty sheets of paper or two phonographs can do. Just because personal teaching is precious and can do what books and apparatus cannot, it should be saved for its peculiar work. The best teacher uses books and appliances as well as his own insights, sympathy and magnetism.' With the development of a range of media and accessibility in libraries and the home, the personal relationships between lecturer and student have more potential for development now than ever before. It is unfortunate that some view lecturing to 200 students as the personal relationship between lecturer and student!

Compare the range of media with the criteria set out on the first page of this chapter. What constraints operate in your institution (e.g. range of facilities, access to facilities, student access, etc.)?

9 MANAGEMENT OF LEARNING — THE PERFORMER

Organisation of Materials for Conventional Methods

In an orchestra (or a play) each performer is required to meld in with the others. The balance of sounds and the emphases of instruments are written by the composer and co-ordinated by the conductor. The individual performer needs to practise his part and to perfect it to enable the group to perform at their best. The part may require new techniques to be learned and tedious practice of difficult parts. The performer has a script or score on which to base his performance. In some performances the script or score is very tightly specified; in others, such as jazz (or free drama), it can be very loosely specified.

Each lecturer is part of a team related to a particular discipline and guides students in their learning. For those leading service courses, mastery of techniques to be used will be the requirement, whilst for those leading final year degree courses some creative ideas based on analysis are needed. All the collection and organisation of resources for the students' learning environment need consideration. It is surprising how many lecturers can be caught out on simple organisation. An unfamiliar room is always worth checking before using.

1. How big is the chalkboard?
2. Is there any chalk and a cleaner?
3. How do the lights switch on and off?
4. Are there any remote controls for screens, ventilation, projectors, television, etc., and if so how do they work?
5. Is there any black-out?
6. What facilities are available?
7. How can facilities be booked and how will they function in the room (e.g. overhead projector, 16 mm projector)?
8. Is there a projection screen?
9. How does one's voice carry in the room?
10. Is there any amplification system, and how does it work?
11. What size of writing is necessary for the chalkboard, the overhead projector? (Try it and find out — make a note on your file of notes.)
12. Is there room for all the students?

13. Is it feasible to re-arrange the seating? (Allow time to replace it afterwards.)

Having found the answers to these questions, the material may need reorganising. For example, a long chalkboard may need sectioning for the arrangement of material, as shown below.

Long chalkboard

A	B	C	D	E	F
List of headings	Material to be developed and not wiped off	Working section 1	Working section 2	Working section 3	Key words 'scribbling pad' for answers to queries

The pattern should be consistent so that students know what to expect; for example what is on sections C, D, and E is going to disappear at some stage, whereas that on A and B is not. A quite different system is necessary with sliding or roller boards where parts are obscured, although available if necessary. Five minutes spent on planning this enables a better performance to be given. Similarly five minutes used at the beginning to rearrange chairs in a smaller room from serried rows to a square, circle or horseshoe arrangement will assist interaction in tutorials, seminars and discussion sessions.(Another five minutes will be necessary at the end to put the chairs back as they were found!)

A brief rehearsal through slides and/or overhead projector transparencies will ensure that all are there and in good condition, and that slides are marked for loading into the projector.

Identification spot in top RH corner facing away from screen

Slides marked as shown are placed in the projector with the spot at the top right facing *away* from the screen. If there is time it is always worthwhile to run through all slides and check that they project the

right way up and the right way round and to re-mark any slides that are incorrectly marked. Slides are better kept in groups or in wallets that fit into a filing cabinet to enable easy access.

Index Card of Four Overhead Projector Transparencies

Overhead projector transparencies are more clumsy to arrange and organise. A simple classification using key words or numbers can be used on each transparency. Index cards are kept with copies of the information (see example below). It is much easier to flick through cards than transparencies. A record of the number and sequence of the transparencies can be made on lecture notes.

Many lecturers find the use of sheets for notes clumsy as a basis for delivery. The use of cards, which are easy to hold in the hand, is a useful substitute. At each point where writing is to be done on the blackboard, the overhead projector or flip chart, a symbol is incorporated to indicate this. Similarly symbols are used to indicate where prepared transparencies (overhead projector or 35 mm) are to be used. For those who prefer a less structured organisation, a patterned note of the type indicted earlier in the book gives freedom of sequencing according to the reactions of and interactions with students.

Even discussions, tutorials and seminars need adequate organisation and preparation. A series of open questions (those starting with 'why', 'what', 'how' are usually more useful because it is not possible to answer 'yes' or 'no'). The questions are held as means of provoking, directing or drawing out comments and to prevent the lecturer dominating the discussion. Even in problem classes there is no need for the lecturer to provide the answers. Judicious use of 'What do you think?' and supportive or non-commital comments interspersed with silences ensure student participation rather than lecturer participation. It is advisable to check resources at least 24 hours before the session with students. Only in this way is it at all possible to alter the sequence because the materials and equipment are not available or in need of replacement.

What about hand-outs? As was stated earlier in the book, there is no prescriptive dogma. It does seem that many students write more

2 ASSESSMENT

2.1 STUDENTS

predictive
absolute
diagnostic
comparative

2.2 ITEM PERFORMANCE CHARACTERISTICS

Norm-referenced

normal
ratio
cardinal

Criterion-referenced

skew
ordinal
nominal

2.3 (5 students x 5 papers data)

I II III IV V

A
B
C
D
E

(overlays for totals, means, s.d. etc)

2.4 PURPOSES OF ASSESSMENT

1. Help students understanding of a subject as a whole

2. Relationship between understanding and indices of competence

3. Measure of personal expression and/or involvement

useful notes if the structure but not the detail, occurs in hand-outs. A hand-out on assessment might be:

Assessment

Student	Course
1. Predictive	Formative
2. Absolute	
3. Diagnostic	Summative
4. Comparative	

The form is identical to the overhead projector transparency indicated on the card shown earlier in the chapter. The spaces on the hand-out enable the student to elaborate and cross-reference as he wishes. Obviously the purpose of the layout should be made clear. For other students even this degree of structuring will present patterns of association which do not fit into their own personal experiences and cognitive structures. So it is advisable to state that this is not the only classification or organisation feasible.

There is not much point in leaving the preparation of hand-outs until 24 hours previously. If you regularly use hand-outs it is more realistic to prepare well in advance — a day spent at the beginning of the academic year organising dates for preparation and putting them in a diary is time well spent. As can be seen, the role of stage manager and property and wardrobe manager is a good theatrical analogy. The careful organisation of scores, music stands and instrument stands is the nearest musical analogy. The organisation can be summarised in the form of a checklist like the one that follows:

1. Are course notes up to date?
2. Are the notes in a form that can easily be used?
3. Are all uses of the chalkboard and projectors cross-referenced?
4. Are all overhead projector transparencies and 35 mm slides in good condition?
5. Are all the transparencies arranged in order ready for use?
6. Are all the 35 mm slides correctly 'spotted'?
7. Have any hand-outs to be updated, modified, prepared and printed?
8. Has the room been checked for facilities (see checklist earlier in chapter)?
9. Have all projectors and equipment required been booked?
10. Do students know format and expectations?
11. Have student pre-requisites been organised and checked?
12. Have pauses and/or light reliefs been built in to help student concentration?
13. Has a brief rehearsal been carried out?

In most of the conventional teaching methods, (the lecture, the problems class and the seminar) the lecturer is often viewed by students and by himself as the virtuoso performer. A soloist needs much more practice and accuracy than a member of an orchestra, a lead-part actor has more impact than a small-part actor, but only by dint of experience, hard work and panache. The lecturer is also a conductor, but the role of conductor is rather different and will be considered in the next chapter.

Organisation on the Day of Performance

If cards or notes are used, not only is it useful to mark the positions where the chalkboard, slides, and overhead projector transparencies are to be used, but also to list these in the correct sequence at the beginning. For example:

A	*Oh: 2.1, 2.4, 2.3, 2.2; HO: 1, 9*			
B	*Assessment*			*1*
C	Oh 2.1 2 bases	— *Student*	*Course*	
D	HO I subdivisions	predictive	formative	
		absolute		
		diagnostic	summative	
		comparative		

Key: Line A. The set of overhead projector transparencies (see diagram on page 93) and hand-outs needed and put in the sequence of use.

Line B. Main heading for chalkboard.

Line C. Use of first overhead transparency.

Line D. Having introduced headings give out hand-out (see below for details).

Elaboration and detail of each sub-heading would follow.

If this card was the first on a lecture of assessment, the overhead projector transparency would be used as a basis to elaborate the structure of the lecture. The associated hand-out would be given out to students. At the top of the card are listed the overhead projector transparencies and hand-outs to be used *in the correct order*.

A quick check through the transparencies and hand-outs before the lecture will check that all is ready. I find it helpful to indicate how much time can be spent on each part of the lecture, with optional parts which can be removed if running behind schedule. For those who are nervous about talking to a group of students, a few deep breaths before going into the room may help considerably. It is also helpful if you can completely tense yourself from head to foot and then gradually relax from the extremities.

If you have a tendency to talk in a monotonous voice then you need to have a note on your cards or sheets to remind you to vary pace, pitch and to use pauses. Have you ever heard and/or seen yourself in action? It is very easy to organise with a camera, a microphone and a video recorder. Voice production is an underestimated science and art. No presenter can expect to be heard without adequate technique. The control of breath, the resonances in the air passages, chest and mouth, the elaborated and correct pronunciation of consonants all help. In most institutions there is a member of staff with expertise in these skills (e.g. a speech therapist, drama specialist). In order to improve performance, practice and exercises are essential.

A further area worth consideration is the use of the eyes. Eye contacts with individual students scattered around the room over a period of time gives students the impressions of (a) a desire by the lecturer to communicate, (b) a feeling of involvement, and not least (c) a wish to stay awake and alert! Facial expressions and gesticulations help to elaborate points. The larger the audience, the more essential it is that these are well rehearsed. With adequate organisation prior to entry, any performer can do his best when actually performing.

Without adequate preparation no performer can give of his best.

For tutorials the preparatory cards and notes need to be different. Most of us need reminders to 'be quiet and listen'. Silences in a discussion are necessary to some extent — it is not the leader's role to fill every minute's silence! It is worth remembering too that not only should the students be satisfied with the learning experience, but also with the lecturer.

Collection of Information for Future Work

It is worth noting down as soon as a session has taken place any reactions from students, any problems that arose, and possible means of overcoming them. Some other suggestions may arise from colleagues. A careful note of these comments is worth adding to the cards or sheets immediately, otherwise there will be no reminders when preparing for successive performances in future years. Some further suggestions for feedback are given in Chapter 12.

10 MANAGEMENT OF LEARNING — THE CONDUCTOR

Organisation of Materials: Variations on Conventional Methods

Whilst many conventional methods are dependent on a virtuoso solo performance, variations on those methods are more akin to the conductor in an orchestra or the producer or director in dramatic performance. The role of the performer is now transferred to the students whom the lecturer coerces, cajoles or encourages to take on the leading roles. The orchestration and the dominations by individual students are the variations in performance, which to an outside observer are produced by each lecturer.

Consider the use of buzz group type lecture sequences. No longer is the control of content and flow entirely in the lecturer's hands. From the material that is available to him he must guide the action as best he can. The technique elaborated on page 49 can be very useful in classification exercises. For example if students are considering assessment procedures, each student is asked to write down what they consider to be the purposes of assessment. When most students have finished writing, pairs are asked to find differences between their contributions. Again on completion groups of four are asked to come to a consensus if possible (it is worth emphasising that in some cases consensus may *not* be possible). On completion each group reports one purpose. With careful planning of the chalkboard (subdivided into at least seven sections to cover the six sub-headings on page 93, and one spare for responses which fall outside the classification, the responses can be grouped, but the headings are not incorporated. When each group has contributed all that they have to offer, students can be asked to see if they can see any sort of pattern. As a pattern evolves headings can be put on each column.

It is clear that a different kind of preparation and organisation is necessary to that in a conventional lecture. The essential features are running to a time schedule and being able to elucidate the meaning behind student statements. Preparatory notes will have the form of the session — i.e. a time schedule, and the classification headings. Not only do the classification headings need to be known by heart, but also practice is needed to classify other people's statements. By asking the same question ('What are the purposes of assessment?' in this case) to students not on that course and to other academics with limited knowledge, practice is gained in classifying statements. A summary overhead projector transparency or 35 mm slide provides an obvious rounding-off point. For more complex questions where opinion needs supplementing with facts a *short* reading list can be given in advance — a hand-out at the end of the previous session.

For problems classes the problems are usually given out a week previously. The sort of questions to consider are:

1. Should the answers be incorporated?
2. Should each student's working be seen (the process)?
3. Should each student see the tutor?
4. Should students work with one another, and, if so how are the groups organised?
5. What is the purpose of the problems class — for students to help one another, for the lecturer to issue a monologue of solutions, or to encourage students to come up with ideas for solutions?
6. What does the student expect at the beginning?
7. What is the role of the lecturer?

Answers to most of these questions need to be clarified before the first problem class in order to set the pattern. The division of time between checking, peer teaching, and use of lecturer as expert may vary from week to week, but the general pattern will be the same. Remembering the role of conductor, the students (not the lecturers) are the performers.

For tutorials and discussion sessions the preparation of materials is just as important. A strategy for organising learning through discussion is given in the book by Hill (1977). This strategy not only incorporates preparation by learners, but also the roles of members of a group. The book itself would act as an excellent basis for the first discussion. If groups are going to meet regularly it is important that each member of the group perceives his role and that of each other member of the group. There is also a suggestion that at the end of each discussion the members of the group evaluate what has taken place and one another's roles on that occasion.

Organisation of Materials: Unconventional Methods

Where new methods are introduced, careful preparation and organis-ation of materials is crucial. Students expect new methods to be well organised and efficiently presented. Inadequate preparation and organisation soon alienate students who are often basically conservative in their approach to learning. Some key questions to be asked of any innovation are:

1. How familiar are students with this method?
2. How can students be helped to cope with an unfamilar method?
3. How easy is any material to access and to use?
4. What help can be given to students to help them in accessing and in using the material?
5. How does the method relate to the rest of the students' course, assessments, assignments, etc.?
6. What happens if something is lost or damaged in use? (e.g. are duplicates available at short notice?)
7. Are students expected to work on their own or in groups?
8. Is any form of de-briefing necessary?
9. Are any supplementary printed materials needed?
10. How long will it take to prepare any materials needed?
11. Who can give any help, assistance or professional advice on the preparation of materials?
12. How easy will it be to modify or update the materials each year?
13. Who checks to see that everything is always there and returned after use?

It is important to remember that the longer the innovation is used by the lecturer, the more assumptions are made about the students' knowledge of it, in spite of the fact that the innovation may still be just as unfamiliar to students in the third year of use as in the first year. A checklist along the lines of the one given above is useful to use each year to ensure that the learner is adequately prepared and informed.

With activities like projects and dissertations it needs to be made clear to students what the requirements and expectations are. Because projects have been used for the last five or ten years it does not mean that this year's group are adequately informed, although we may be tired of explaining year after year. In many departments an elaborate procedure has been set up to ensure that the assumptions of familarity do not occur. An extensive checklist is used in one department (Black, 1975) to ensure that the student and his tutor do communicate on all the important aspects and that they agree what the project is attempting to do. If this is not written down at the beginning it is so easy to raise or lower expectations without either party explicitly agreeing. A project or dissertation is just as much a learning experience as an assessment procedure. Like all learning experiences it should be well organised. Like all assessment procedures it needs careful preparation and management.

Organisation of Examinations, Tests, Assignments, etc.

There are two roles in this area of organisation, (a) the collection of individual questions to assemble the assessments, and (b) the design of questions and the design of mark schemes. In many examinations and tests there is a choice of questions. These questions often carry equal marks but there is no systematic attempt to check that the questions are equal in difficulty. For a really systematic method of checking examination questions and syllabus it is necessary to build a matrix, for example, using the chapter headings of this book for topics where the numbers represent imaginary question numbers.

LEVELS TOPICS	Knowledge recall	Application of knowledge	Simple problem solving	Complex problem solving	Original ideas
Educational materials	1	1			
Communication		2	2		
Process of Learning					3

Topics or sections of the syllabus can be used as bases. These topics or sections could either be equal in length of learning time or deliberately weighted. The levels will be on some basis such as those described in the cognitive levels in Chapter 4. Questions can then be checked against this matrix in order to ensure adequate syllabus cover (if there is a choice), and no duplication. The levels of learning being tested across questions should also be checked. The wording of individual questions needs checking by someone else. How do they interpret the question? What emphases do they expect to be in an answer? It is worth keeping a careful record of questions used, problems that arise in interpretation and students' weaknesses (for more details see page 123).

When using multiple choice questions, or other styles of question where students select answers, design is very important. Some considerations are:

1. What information is given to students on how to answer (even simple things like the use of a tick, cross, or underlining to indicate the right answer)?
2. Is there a separate answer sheet?
3. How many answers can be chosen?
4. Are students expected to guess when they do not answer or to leave the question blank?
5. Are there any penalties for choosing the incorrect option?

An example is given below.

For all questions students must select ONE answer which they consider to be the most correct. Students will be penalised for choosing more than one answer. The appropriate option is marked on the answer sheet by circling the letter of that option.

Suppose Q 107 was:

107   The capital of England is
       A Paris
       B Winchester
       C London
       D Birmingham

The correct answer is 'London' so this would be shown on the answer sheet as

•
•
•

106	A	B	C	D	E	F
107	A	B	Ⓒ	D	E	F
108	A	B	C	D	E	F

•
•
•

In order to set multiple choice questions it is worth writing a simple short answer question first which can then be tried with a sample of students. The distractors are chosen for the multiple choice question by using the most common student errors. The performance of the question is checked and a record card kept for future reference on each item. In addition comments from other lecturers and from students are worth recording for modifications in wording, design and layout. Some other suggestions on the use of the results of student's attempts on assessments is included in Chapter 12.

11 MANAGEMENT OF LEARNING — THE COMPOSER

Organisation of Thoughts

In many books a variety of techniques are elaborated for designing courses and learning materials such as network analysis, flowcharts, algorithms etc. The role of the producer of learning materials can be compared to that of the author, composer or playwright. As such the producer's role can be looked upon as applying a systematic procedure to a problem-solving process. This process can be simplified into the list shown in the figure below. The first three elements are primarily heuristic procedures upon which analysis and synthesis can be based. The use of the techniques listed in the first paragraph are a means of processing data, demonstrating the results of a heuristic process, or of retrieving data. The tools are primarily analytic tools not design tools.

Certainly it is worth displaying thoughts on paper in some systematic way. In this book the use of patterned notes has been elaborated. These are a useful way of demonstrating initial heuristic solution strategies to problems. A more rigorous presentation requires the relative sequencing of elements of learning based on content or level. For these, more sophisticated display techniques highlight different procedural problems.

From the illumination of these problems an alternative strategy may be necessary. The tools used are not creative although they can aid the heuristic procedure. The tools sometimes enable the rules and traditional relationships to be emphasised. It may be that the innovation is deliberately attempting to break down these traditional orthodoxies, in which case the tools become a hindrance. Nevertheless systematic procedures still have a role. The evaluation of an alternative strategy is essential. In addition the alternative strategy may require

Application of Systems Procedures to a Problem-solving process involving analysis and synthesis

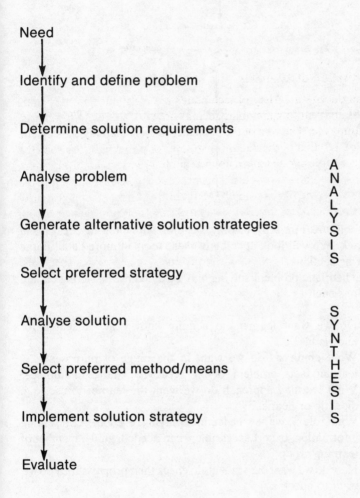

Need

↓

Identify and define problem

↓

Determine solution requirements

↓

Analyse problem

↓

Generate alternative solution strategies

↓

Select preferred strategy

↓

Analyse solution

↓

Select preferred method/means

↓

Implement solution strategy

↓

Evaluate

A
N
A
L
Y
S
I
S

S
Y
N
T
H
E
S
I
S

new pre-requisites which will also need investigating. The relationships can be shown as follows:

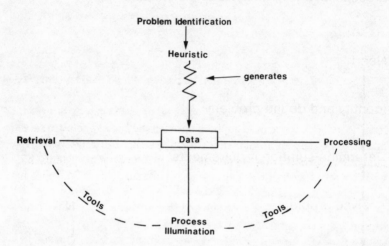

The tools are primarily display systems with built-in checks and feedback. We will look at some of these tools in more detail in the following sections.

The heuristic problem-solving may be aided by answering certain questions such as:

1. Do we want learners to acquire knowledge or search for knowledge?
2. What emphasis do we want in the range of purposes (e.g. learning facts, problem solving, creativity, change in attitude)?
3. What learning approach do we want the learner to use (e.g. didactic or heuristic)?
4. What role do we see the lecturer playing (e.g. expert presenting information, expert accessible when needed, guide, member of learning group)?
5. How do we want our students to check their progress? (Or do we want to check it?)

The answers to questions of this type give the parameters for decision-making. For example one clear point that will emerge is that some students view their learning as a means to an end (e.g. a career in medicine, engineering, social work), in which case the approach may be job or career-oriented, highly structured, didactic, and based in the real world, whereas other students do not view their learning as a means to an end (e.g. courses in philosophy, theology, literature, history), in which case the approach may be based on personal exploration and unstructured materials. However there is no reason why the approaches need to be oriented as described. These are the traditional orthodox approaches. There is little or no evidence to show that either is more effective in its context.

The decisions are also related to independence in learning as outlined earlier in the book. In which spheres should students have independence? Strategy, sequence, content, or assessment? If students have no independence in any sphere how can they be expected to solve problems outside the formal educational system? Fortunately individual human beings are more adaptable than educational systems, but with more adaptation of the system, individuals may improve in adapting to the outside world.

The decisions on the questions and the problems posed above are useful when using patterned notes or any of the other techniques outlined in this chapter. Some of the methods may highlight problems which will require modifications of the original decisions but not fundamental changes, unless the constraints have been ignored. Constraints include the institution, any external bodies which exert pressure (e.g. professional organisations, examining boards, etc.). Other constraints that often cannot be changed are:

(1) facilities (e.g. laboratory space, equipment);
(2) learning spaces (e.g. size, furniture arrangements);
(3) assessment procedures;
(4) ethos of the institution;
(5) finance;
(6) staffing (including technical and secretarial);
(7) attitudes of colleagues;
(8) requirements of professional bodies;
(9) books;
(10) time.

Flowcharts

Under this heading I include network analysis, information mapping, critical path analysis, program evaluation and review technique

(PERT). The primary constraint of these methods is that the initial problem must have been identified prior to use (i.e. the first three stages of the problem-solving process delineated at the begining of this chapter). Only brief outlines are given here; for further details consult the relevant references both in this chapter and in the annotated bibliography.

Simple flowcharts show the relationship between parts, for example:

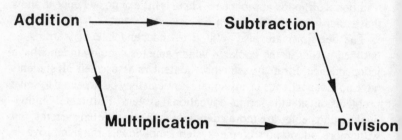

shows a very simple relationship. The decision about whether to do subtraction or multiplication first would be based on further sub-division of the elements or on the basis of experience. The sequence as shown is based on decisions made prior to drawing the flowchart, that addition is the basis of subtraction and of multiplication. A flowchart can be produced in any direction (e.g. horizontally, left to right or vice versa, or vertically, top to bottom or vice versa). As the flowchart gets larger it is often more convenient to use numbers to show the elements, thus reducing the size of the chart. A more complex chart may look like:

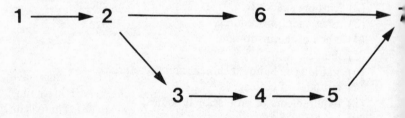

where the numbers represent the activities.

In network analysis the lines represent the activities and the numbered circles the ends of activities (nodes), as for example:

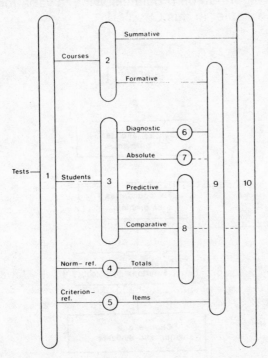

The relationships (and therefore the longest path, i.e. the route with the largest number of nodes), can be determined, Taken a stage further still, it is possible to estimate probable maximum and minimum times for each activity. The programme can be evaluated and reviewed to determine the critical path (i.e. the maximum time) and the likely errors in estimates of various parts. Obviously decisions must have been taken to determine the first network, from which errors in routing, timing and interrelationships can be clarified and altered. There is no reason why the flow diagrams, networks, etc. cannot be shown to the learner. The learner can also use the techniques actively to plan his own schedules and learning. Patterned notes are in themselves a rudimentary form of network or flowchart.

Algorithmic Techniques

Algorithmic techniques require a decision route — according to the answer given in a previous section of the algorithm. A simple example is shown below:

A simple algorithm on problem-solving (a variation on the list shown earlier in this Chapter)

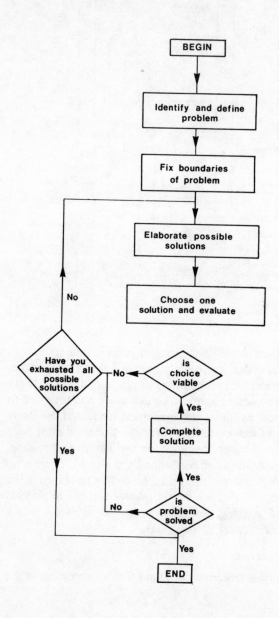

The route is straightforward through rectangular boxes, but at a diamond-shaped box a decision has to be made. If the solution being investigated is not viable, the route is taken to another diamond-shaped box with a simple yes/no decision. A true algorithm will eventually take the user to the 'end' box. Landa (1974) argues that this technique is of more use to learners in organising their problem-solving strategies than to designers. However algorithms do have a very obvious use when temporary learning is required to solve a particular problem. Many government leaflets would be more helpful if presented in algorithmic form than in prose (especially when the prose sometimes amounts to 160 words in one sentence!). For learners in further and higher education algorithms are very suitable for checking problems arising in the use of equipment. An example was quoted earlier in relation to the use of computer terminals by students.

Audio Visual Materials

The strategies vary from audio tapes for language laboratories, synchronised still pictures and audio tape, to film and television. Careful planning is essential for materials which require the production of a sequence of spoken word and/or visual materials.

The spoken word must be genuine conversational English (or foreign language) not the spoken written word. In the written word the range of vocabulary, and in particular the range of specialist vocabulary, is extensive. The reader is helped by the structure of the sentences and if he does not understand what he reads, he can refer back. In the conversational and spoken word there is more redundancy of words and less structure. In order to get a script for the spoken word there are several possible techniques, two of which will be briefly outlined. These techniques are as applicable in the lecture as they are in audio recordings, film or television. Before using either of these techniques:

1. Get to know your own voice and its idiosyncracies.
2. Develop a system for marking rises in pitch, increase in pace, pauses, etc. in your script.
3. Use silences as well as speech — pauses encourage thinking and concentration, if well chosen.
4. If the recording is to be used with a synchronised audio and visual presentation, remember that a finite time is necessary for the picture to change either manually or automatically.

The first technique is tedious, but does ensure that the spoken word is used:

1. Take a tape recorder and talk about the topic as though you were describing it to a *friend (not* a colleague). It doesn't matter how many mistakes you make — this is a rough version. Note where you do make mistakes since this may suggest parts where you felt that you were not explaining properly. If you can actually talk to a friend whilst explaining you are more likely to observe their reactions and modify your talk accordingly.

2. On completion listen to the recording and write down exactly what you said, leaving large gaps between lines.

3. Now listen to the recording with the script. Mark on the script any place about which you are unhappy and note the position on the recording (either with the counter number, using zero at the start of your talk, by marking the tape with a small piece of paper on reel to reel machines, or with a small mark of white paint on cassette recordings). Also mark the script with a symbol for small pauses (I use △) and larger pauses (PAUSE). From a learner's point of view the pauses and their length are as important as the emphases. Any place where responses will be required can also be marked (RESPONSE).

4. Re-write all sections where modifications were necessary; check the new section against the original recording.

5. Add in any questions necessary to elicit a response. The script is now ready for re-recording.

6. Re-record, only this time record under conditions as ideal as possible on a good quality reel to reel machine. If at all possible have expert technical assistance and use an acoustically treated room. If you make a mistake, stop, note the place and immediately correct it. After recording the master tape can be physically edited, removing all mistakes and extending or contracting pauses as necessary.

7. If students are required to respond on a section of tape and to compare their performance, check the way that the playback machine works before organising this part.

8. If extra pauses are to be built in, for example for visual changes, consider a good point to motivate the change — it does not have to be the end of a sentence — the picture may act as motivation for words that follow (see later in this chapter).

9. It is worth adding some indication that the recording has

come to an end. Some people like to use music, but this is fraught with copyright problems. A simple method is to add the statement 'This is the end of this recording, will you please re-wind the tape.'

10. Try the recording out with some students to get their reaction.

11. Make a copy of the master recording for actual use. Never use the master copy. If cassettes are being used, do not forget to punch out the two lugs to ensure that the recording is not easily wiped.

The second method is much simpler, but less accurate. Write very brief outlines or key words on cards or on paper. These act as cues to which you talk, but prevent you from reading. When this has been done, have a trial recording to see if you need any further promptings. If you are satisfied with this, pick up at point 5 on the list above.

These methods are all right where the material is primarily in the spoken word. For a combination of audio and visual, techniques like the one below help to produce a smoother flow. If you have no experience in this type of work, draw up a simple story board as shown.

STORY BOARD (TV AND FILM PRODUCTIONS)

TITLE:

Sponsor / Originator   School

References   Date   Time

Location   Equipment
                              (Brief Summary)

Shot No	Camera		Details, Comments, Notes, etc.

The camera column will be referred to for television and film productions. For synchronised audio and visual productions it is not used. In the rectangles a sketch of the picture to use is shown. In the column on the right hand side the script and any comments about pauses, responses, etc. are shown. (For example, some machines have a built-in system whereby the machine stops until the student re-activates it. If this facility is to be used it must be marked. If a subsidiary printed sheet is to be used this also needs noting.)

Two immediate checks can be carried out with each visual: (a) that there are not too few words and (b) that there are not too many! Provided that there is not a continual change of picture or a continual sequence of long spells of talking with few visuals, variations are less important. The next thing to check is the motivation for each change in picture and for the development of the words. Try to put yourself in the viewer's position — he should not be saying to himself 'Why on earth has this picture changed?' — it is obvious that the change should have some reason. A simple example is as follows. A shot is changing from a picture of London to one of New York; the commentary on London's churches has not yet finished and whilst the last sentence is still being spoken a picture of New York skyscrapers appears. The viewer will not now hear what is being said about London. If after completing the talk about London, the commentary starts about the style of building in New York, then the picture can change — the viewer has a cue. An alternative way would be to complete the talking on London and have a short pause when the picture changes — the viewer now expects to hear about New York. In the first case the spoken word acted as motivation for the picture and in the second case vice versa. If you are in any doubt, watch some good television programmes or films and analyse the motivation techniques used. This is an art and it is the sort of area where professional advice is most helpful.

If you are still not happy, borrow a simple portable video recorder and camera. Assemble sketches or photographs that will be used and put together a very rough version of your story board. Now get some students to view this with you and note down their comments, problems, etc. Modify the story board accordingly. Any photographs etc. can now be taken. The audio recording can be made as already outlined.

For television the procedure is not very different if a production is involved. It is essential that the limitations of the equipment and space are carefully considered. For example the close-up shots will be limited by the type of zoom lens, the lighting available, the ability of the cameraman (there is little point in having a close-up shot which is not tightly in focus) and the quality of the video recorders.

Other factors are the number of cameras available that can be used simultaneously, and the editing facilities available. If more than one camera is available, careful scripting may be necessary. The story board that you have developed will have to be discussed with professionals who know the limitations and idiosyncracies of their own equipment. Many improvements may well be suggested. It is worthwhile asking for a rough assembly in order to get some idea of the final presentation before getting involved in the arduous task of making a recording — a twenty-minute programme that is well scripted may well take up to a day to make. There are several relatively simple books which elaborate some of the details of television production (for example Davies, 1974; Millerson, 1976).

If television is being used for immediate replay much planning is still involved, for example how feasible is what you want in terms of the facilities available? Again a rough run-through is well worth the effort to iron out a variety of problems that may arise. In addition the rooms and facilities that are available for replay must be considered. Do you want individuals or pairs to view their own performance separately?

Film involves a more long-term investment. It is not possible to see the results immediately. The selection and sequencing of shots is not only done in the filming, but also in the editing. A collection of neutral but relevant shots is necessary to enable editing to be more precise. If synchronised sound is required (for example a person talking to the camera, called 'lip synchronisation'), special equipment is necessary. Outdoor filming is heavily dependent on weather for adequate contrasts in lighting. Indoor filming will probably require supplementary lighting. For educational films a detailed script is essential, otherwise considerable waste of film stock (expensive) and time (even more expensive) is likely to occur. Again a rough assembly using portable television equipment will give some idea of the visual impact. The use of professional advice and assistance is essential if a master 16 mm film is to be made, from which copies will be printed.

Printed Materials

For some reason it is often assumed that printed materials do not require the same sort of preparation as audio visual materials. If attention is not given to layout and format the impact will be considerably reduced. A typical problem, especially when using typewritten material, is the correct use of spaces and gaps. Double-spaced typewritten material is a little too far apart for easy reading and single spaced too close together. An added problem with lithographic procedures is the amount of reduction. With large reductions it may be necessary to split the page into two columns to give easy scanning when reading. If your institution has a qualified printing officer he will be able to give some guidance.

Boundary lines for typing make the typist's job easier to ensure relatively even presentation at both ends of the line.

Tables need careful consideration. Most tables contain far too much data. The decision on labelling and which to use as the rows and the columns is also crucial to ease of reading.

Large bold diagrams are usually better, even if hand-drawn, than minute detailed diagrams. Careful consideration to framing and position are needed if the diagram does not occupy a separate page. Space around a diagram helps to emphasis it. Diagrams should be very close to the text to which they refer.

A draft layout, even roughly pasted up from handwriting, helps to give some idea of the impact and the need for spaces.

The need for careful design is essential for distant study systems and for support materials to go with audio visual presentations (something for students to take away!).

Computer-Assisted and Computer-Managed Learning

A complete introduction to the field of educational computing is given by Rushby (1979) in the first book in this series, *An Introduction to Educational Computing.* What follows is a short personal account of this area of relatively new techniques and strategies in learning. Computer-assisted learning is where the computer is used actively with the student either to interact with his responses (a sort of sophisticated programmed learning) or to provide simulations of real systems. In the latter case the student can investigate the effects of changing or modifying parameters in a system (for example in a building structure, a chemical plant or a management game). The design of any such system is dependent on computer programs, storage facilities and terminals. Once a student has overcome the fear of the computer system and becomes involved in the problem the motivation seems to be good, presumably because of the rapid response and interaction. It is at the briefing stage, and ensuring that the student interface with the computer is uncomplicated, that extra attention is needed once the program has been devised or installed.

One of the main uses of computer-managed learning in higher education has been with diagnostic testing. The detailed design of questions (often in multiple choice format) and of the computer program has taken most of the effort. However if diagnostic testing is to be effective considerable effort needs to go into other elements of the system:

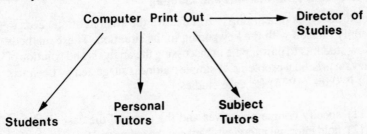

The handing of a large sheaf of computer print-out to each of those shown is not sufficient. Who wants what information? Surely all do not want all the information? What information and data would be useful? Having got the data what action is taken by whom? Without a very careful consideration of the communication end of the project all the effort in designing the questions and the computer program is wasted. A very simple set of decisions might be:

Students receive a copy of their personal incorrect answers and the appropriate correct answers; for learning to occur, access to the original questions is essential; a total mark and a mean or median for the whole group may be useful on the basis of groups of questions (e.g. on one topic/subject area).

Personal Tutors receive all their students' data; a copy of the question paper; an instruction sheet (short and simple!) on how to use the data with students.

Subject Tutors receive all the students' data on their group of questions; some simple statistical data; an instruction sheet on interpretation and use of the data (others would include a recommendation to give students copies of the question paper at least in class, checking mistakes).

Directors of Studies receive a comprehensive detailed print-out with checks of individual question responses, student data, grouped question data. This lecturer has the key data for disputes and for any approach by any student or member of staff.

It is necessary for students to know how they go about using the information they get, who will help them with problems and how lecturers will cover their subject areas. The basic expectation in diagnostic testing is to help students over their problems and also to highlight these problems.

Case Studies, Simulations and Gaming

For these types of learning to be effective the student often needs to identify himself with the key person in the situation. These methods allow students to participate in discussing the analysis and solution of relevant practical problems. A simple routine is suggested by Leenders and Erskine (1973) for case studies:

(1) specify course objectives and the place of the case study;
(2) hold informal interviews between the writer and the organisation on which the case will be based;
(3) prepare a one-page outline of a mini-case.

The mini-case acts as a basis for decisions to be made: (a) whether the case meets the course objectives, (b) the feasibility of development and (c) the permission to progress using pseudonyms and appropriate disguises.

Once a decision has been made to progress, there are three areas in which further decisions are needed.

(1) how analytical the case should be (a spectrum from 'Here is a problem and a solution, do they fit?' to 'Here is a situation, what are the problems, what are the solutions?');
(2) what conceptual levels should be involved (from 'almost everyone will grasp the concept' to 'extensive clarification and lecturer involvement');
(3) how detailed the presentation should be (from 'little extraneous material to 'a large amount of extraneous material').

These decisions are as applicable in simulations and gaming situations as in case studies. The main constraints are time (for student use and for design) and resources available.

12 MANAGEMENT OF LEARNING — THE CRITIC

The Problems of Noise

All communciations suffer from 'noise' — the unwanted background and interference. Noise is caused not only by poor production techniques but also by incorrect assumptions about the learner's knowlege (both technical and of the medium) and past experience. Any design is inevitably a compromise because each learner will have different past experiences. It is essential that the problems of noise are investigated and as far as possible eliminated. The reduction of noise will certainly reduce the mismatch between the lecturer (the transmitter), the transmission, and the learner (the receiver). One essential purpose of evaluation is to reduce the noise and the mismatch. Perhaps as little as 2 per cent of optimum capacity is used in most learning channels. The purpose of educational technology should be to improve the proportion of capacity in use to at least 10 per cent initially. One essential means to improve capacity is by feedback of information.

Although extensive research on learning is being conducted in many areas, the lecturer himself has many means at his disposal to find how the course in which he is involved is progressing. Is it effective? What do we mean by effective? Each individual lecturer may have a different emphasis in his understanding of the word effective. 'Effective' may include:

(1) a good personal performance (e.g. voice, presentation);
(2) students learning a lot of factual data;
(3) students getting a good set of notes;
(4) students enjoying the course;
(5) students going on and carrying out follow up work with or without further encouragement — solving problems, reading references, asking questions;
(6) students achieving the goals laid down for the course;
(7) students being very interested or excited about the course.

Further statements could be added by using the checklist in Chapter 11.

In order to make decisions on effectiveness it is necessary to have some basis for the decisions. Possible sources of information are:

(1) academic colleagues;
(2) students;
(3) examination answers;
(4) tests;
(5) questionnaires;
(6) free responses;
(7) video or audio recordings of the course;
(8) one's own opinions;
(9) observation.

If the collection of this information is systematic the detailed modifications of courses can be worked out more thoroughly (the 'hole plugging' and 'patching' of Chapter 1). Let us consider each of these sources of information in detail.

Academic Colleagues

Discussions with colleagues about a course or a lecture are often very rewarding in ideas. Each member of a group of lecturers had one lecture video recorded. The group viewed each recording, their comments to one another were not only critical, but enthusiastic — 'That's a good idea', 'I didn't know that you did that' — leading to more elaboration of interrelationships between courses. Tutors can provide valuable information to the lecturer responsible for a course by reporting problems raised by students in tutorials.

Students

When any part of a course is not clear many students will ask questions indicating their level of confusion. It is worth inserting a comment in the lecture or course notes immediately. Students will often agree to discuss a course or a lecture quite openly with a lecturer, either as a whole group or a small group of representatives. The opening question for such a meeting needs to be along the lines of 'What is your reaction to this course?' or more specifically 'How have you understood this course?' This type of question allows students to emphasise the difficulties and the good points that *they* found. An audio recording of the meeting enables an analysis to be carried out after the discussion (for example 'How leading were my questions?'), but is very time consuming. Many of the other methods discussed use information from students.

Examination Answers

These can give most valuable information. Which questions did most student avoid? Which questions or parts of questions did many students get wrong? A systematic but brief analysis gives clear indicators of problem areas. Interviews with students may illuminate the causes of some of the problems.

Tests

Short answer tests, multiple choice tests or essay tests can give useful information, particularly if they are for the students' benefit and not for classification or qualification purposes. The tests give information to students on their own weaknesses and to lecturers on weaknesses across students. They can be used when students arrive in order to elucidate weaknesses or during the course to show problem areas. The tests can be printed. A much less elaborate method was given in an earlier chapter of key words displayed using the overhead projector, where students were required to write for a couple of minutes on each word.

Questionnaires

Many types of questionnaire can be used, but great care is needed in their design (Oppenheim (1966) is a good book to consult). If students know that a questionnaire will be taken seriously, they will generally fill it in seriously. It is often worthwhile discussing some of the problems brought up by students with a small group. A section at the beginning of the questionnaire for general reactions and a section at the end asking for suggestions for future years give students the opportunity to express their opinions. The questions tend to be biased to what one wants to know, which may exclude some of their opinions. In general there is no need for highly sophisticated questionnaires to be used for the purposes of feedback to individual lecturers. If a department operates a systematic feedback system this can be designed with the aid of students, who will be more aware of what the student group may want to include.

Free Responses

These have the advantage over questionnaires that the student can express his own opinions and problems. A typical approach would be to ask students to write two sides of A4 paper giving their opinions of the course. No more indicators need be given by the lecturer even if requested. A systematic analysis of these responses emphasises problem areas, by looking for clusters of statements that are related to one another.

Video or Audio Recordings of Lectures, Seminars, etc.

In most institutions these can easily be arranged. The recording is viewed or heard and notes taken of problems arising; these problems are added to the notes of the lecture, seminar, etc. It is often helpful to discuss these recordings with a colleague who may well be able to offer advice.

One's Own Opinions

A lecturer has opinions about the way in which a course is progressing. These are worth keeping a note of, as suggested in Chapter 9.

Observation

Have you looked at students' notes? Have you listened to their discussions with one another? The information gleaned about their view of what has been covered in lectures is most illuminating!

The Use of Resources

A key constraint in much development and innovation is continuing and higher education is lack of staff and finance. How often is a serious look taken at the cost in material resources and of staff of providing learning? How cost effective is a lecture? Is the use of television really inordinately expensive? Whatever method is being used, a careful look at the use of resources often pays dividends., What would be the effect of reducing staff-student contact by, say, two or three hours each week and ensuring that that time was spent by the lecturers in preparing materials for students' use (say, for example, work-sheets) and marking associated assignments? The students would be expected to carry out the work during those extra two or three hours. Where is the boundary between cost and effectiveness?

From an institutional point of view these are very important decisions. If a move is made away from lectures to work-sheets it is probable that less lecture room space will be needed, but that more library space will be needed. Space provision is part of the costs.

The role of critic usually leads to action, which may be a patching exercise or a re-design exercise. The critic may be oneself or colleagues or students. In a systematic procedure there is a complete loop, because the resulting action takes us back to the role of composer, performer and conductor.

BIBLIOGRAPHY

Abercrombie, M.L.J., 1960, *The Anatomy of Judgement: an Investigation in to the Processes of Perception and Reasoning* (Penguin, Harmondsworth). This book is still a classic in the field of free group discussion.

——, 1974, *Aims and Techniques of Group Teaching* (Society for Research into Higher Education, Guildford). An outline of the ways in which group teaching functions, based on experimental evidence collected by the author over many years.

Abt, C.C., 1970, *Serious Games* (The Viking Press, New York), p. 176 ff. A book covering the art and science of games that simulate life, in industry, government, education, and personal relations; interpreted with examples.

Adderley, K., 1975, *Project Methods in Higher Education* (Society for Research into Higher Education, London). A survey and a guideline for the use and assessment of project learning.

Bartlett, F.C., 1932, *Remembering: A Study in Experimental and Social Psychology* (Cambridge University Press, London). A classic study on the basic elements of remembering based on experimental work.

Beard, R., 1972, *Teaching and Learning in Higher Education* (Penguin, Harmondsworth). A survey of the present state of the art. (Unfortunately out of print at present.)

Beard, R., Healey, F.G. and Holloway, P.J., 1973, *Objectives in Higher Education* (Society for Research into Higher Education, Guildford). The application of objectives in universities in the UK. A good basic reader for anyone interested in objectives.

Black, J., 1975, 'Allocation and Assessment of Project Work in the Final Year of the Engineering Degree Course at the University of Bath', *Assessment in Higher Education, 1*(1), pp.35–53. A detailed outline of a systematic approach to the organisation and assessment of learning through projects.

Bligh, D.A., 1972, *'What's the Use of Lectures?'* (Penguin, Harmondsworth) (at present out of print). An analysis of the role of the lecture and a variety of other methods of learning. It includes suggestions for preparation of a variety of styles of lecturing. The book is based on a comprehensive survey of available research at that time.

Bligh, D.A., Ebrahim, N., Jaques, D. and Piper,D.W., 1976, *Teaching Students* (University of Exeter, Exeter University Teaching Services, Exeter). An excellent survey of the available literature on teaching, learning and assessment in higher education.

Block, J.H. (ed.), 1971, *Mastery Learning: Theory and Practice* (Holt, Rinehart and Winston, New York). A short collection of papers by the main advocates of a mastery approach to learning.

Bloom, B.S. (ed.), *Taxonomy of Educational Objectives: Handbook 1, The Cognitive Domain* (Longmans, London). The basis of many uses of educational objectives, giving a classification system based on many hundreds of examples.

Broadbent, D.E., 1956, *Perception and Communication* (Pergamon, London). A work that in spite of being over twenty years old is well worth reading; based on experimental data.

Bruner, J.S., 1960, *The Process of Education* (Harvard University Press, Cambridge, Mass.). A classic in the area of processes of learning rather than objectives/end point approach.

Bruner, J.S., Goodnow, J.J. and Austin, G.A., 1956, *A Study of Thinking* (Wiley, New York). An attempt to investigate and suggest the ways in which learners think.

Buckingham, D.J. and Jones, M.H., 1976, 'Visual Communication in Engineering Science', *British Journal of Educational Technology*, *2*(1), pp.48–56. Use of videotape, synchronised tape slide in an engineering course. Outline of early stages in the development of a system.

Carpenter, E., 1967, *Oh What a Blow That Phantom Gave Me* (Paladin, St. Albans, UK). A multi cultural look at how media change people and people change media; based on work carried out by the author in Papua and New Guinea.

Cherry, C., 1966, *On Human Communication* (The M.I.T. Press, Cambridge, Mass.). An in-depth study of a variety of aspects of human communication: speech, logic of communication, cognition and recognition.

Cockburn, B. and Ross, A., 1977, *Lecturecraft* (School of Education, University of Lancaster (Teaching in Higher Education Series No. 1), Lancaster). A pragmatic approach to lecturing.

——, 1977, *Why Lecture?* (School of Education, University of Lancaster (Teaching in Higher Education Series No. 2), Lancaster). A philosophical discussion on the possible outcome and methods of organising for particular circumstances. Some guidance is also given on the use of hand-outs.

——, 1977, *Working Together* (School of Education, University of Lancaster (Teaching in Higher Education Series No. 3), Lancaster). The philosophical basis of group discussion and the way in which groups behave.

——, 1977, *Participatory Discussion* (School of Education, University of Lancaster (Teaching in Higher Education Series No. 4), Lancaster). A pragmatic approach to developing discussion groups in which all contribute. In particular the book deals with factors that encourage and constrain group discussion.

——, 1977, *A Kind of Learning* (School of Education, University of Lancaster (Teaching in Higher Education Series No. 5), Lancaster). This book covers general observations on the types of learning that groups can undertake successfully.

——, 1977, *Patterns and Procedures* (School of Education, University of Lancaster (Teaching in Higher Education Series No. 6), Lancaster). Mainly tips on the management and organisation of different kinds of group arrangements associated with definitions of the arrangements.

——, 1977, *Inside Assessment* (School of Education, University of Lancaster (Teaching in Higher Education Series No. 7), Lancaster). The book is primarily aimed at finals examinations, although it does deal with purposes of assessment and the communication of those purposes to students.

——, 1977, *Essays* (School of Education, University of Lancaster (Teaching in Higher Education Series No. 8), Lancaster). The broad spectrum of situations, in which essays are used in higher education, is covered in this book. The material is well selected and presented.

Collier, K.G. (ed.), 1974, *Innovation in Higher Education* (National Foundation for Educational Research, Slough). Gives details of some innovatory projects in several British universities.

Cornwall, M.G., 1975, 'Authority *v.* Experience in Higher Education', *Universities Quarterly, 19*(3), pp.272–98. An outline of the project orientation in some continental universities.

Cox, G. and Collins, H., 1975, 'Who Cheats? Who Cares?', *Assessment in Higher Education, 1*(1), pp.13–34. A comparison of cheating, plagiarism and other methods of improving performance. Associated with the paper is the outline of results of a survey of industry and commerce on their methods of selecting graduates.

Cox, R., 1967, 'Examinations and Higher Education: a Survey of the Literature', *Universities Quarterly*, June 1967, pp.200–16. A comprehensive, although dated, survey of examining methods. (There are also other papers worth attention in the same issue.)

Davies, D., 1974, *The Grammar of Television Production* (Barrie and Jenkins, London). A very clear simply presented basic reader on professional television production.

Davies, I.K., 1971, *The Management of Learning* (McGraw Hill, London). A systems approach to the organisation and management of learning.

——, 1976, *Objectives in Curriculum Development* (McGraw Hill, London). A well organised book which looks at the range of possibilities of a variety of styles of objectives.

Davies, T.C., 1978, *Open Learning Systems for Mature Students* (Council for Educational Technology, London). The book outlines the present position in the UK with brief reports on existing systems for non-degree work. A series of proposals are given on the way forward.

Davies, W.J.K., 1978, *Implementing Individualised Learning* (Council for Educational Technology, London). A collection of ideas, suggestions, routines and management procedures for individualised learning.

De Bono, E., 1970, *Lateral Thinking: A Textbook of Creativity* (Ward Lock, London). An interesting approach to unconventional thinking and its role in creativity.

Dowdeswell, W.H. and Harris, N.D.C., 1979, *Projects in University Science* in McNally, D. (ed.) *Learning Strategies in University Science* (University of Cardiff Press, Cardiff). A short outline of suggestions for managing and organising projects in university science; based on evidence available.

Dubin, R. and Taveggia, T.C. 1968, *The Teaching Learning Paradox* (University of Oregon Center for the Advanced Study of Educational Administration, Oregon). A concise example of the 'black-box' approach to learning; you can measure what goes in and what comes out but not what occurs inside.

Educational Services Bulletin, 1977, 'Students' Views of Assessment in Engineering' in *Educational Services Bulletin No. 20*, pp.7–10 (Educational Services Unit, University of Bath, Bath, UK). Students' views on the assessment procedures used on their courses.

Entwistle, N. and Hounsell, D., 1975, *How Students Learn*

(Institute for Research and Development in Post Compulsory Education, University of Lancaster, Lancaster). A collection of extracts from classic papers on a variety of aspects of learning selected for the non-specialist reader. Authors of the papers include Ausubel, Broadbent, Bruner, Gagne, Marton, Rogers, Skinner.

Entwistle, N. and Percy, K., 1974, 'Critical Thinking or Conformity? An Investigation of the Aims and Outcomes of Higher Education' in Page, C.F. and Gibson, J. (eds.) *Research into Higher Education 1973* (Society for Research into Higher Education, Guildford). This paper gives the results of part of a large study carried out on study methods and student characteristics.

Entwistle, N. and Wilson, J., 1977, *Degrees of Excellence: The Academic Achievement Game* (Hodder and Stoughton, London). A detailed study of the types of students that are successful in academic studies.

Falk, B. and Kwong, L.D., 1971, *The Assessment of University Teaching* (Society for Research into Higher Education, Guildford). An early book giving suggestions on means of evaluating university teaching.

Gagné, R.M., 1976, *The Conditions of Learning* (Holt, Rinehart and Winston, London). A systematic approach to learning based on a behavioural approach.

——, 1972, 'Domains of Learning', *Interchange, 3*(1), pp.1–8. Gagné's attempt to outline domains of learning — a variation from the affective/cognitive/psychomotor model of Bloom, Krathwohl and their co-workers.

Gibbs, G., 1976, *Learning to Study: A Guide to Running Group Sessions* (Open University Institute of Educational Technology, Milton Keynes). A useful guide for running groups on study methods. The group method is based on group interaction and not on an expert giving his ideas. (An extended version will be published by the Open University Press, probably in 1979.)

Goldschmid, B. and Goldschmid, M.L., 1973, 'Modular Instruction in Higher Education: A Review' *Higher Education, 2*, pp.15–32. An outline of modular methods in higher education with a good collection of further references.

——, 1974, 'Individualising Instruction in Higher Education: A Review', *Higher Education, 3,* pp.1–24. An easy to read analysis of individualised methods with an extensive range of references.

——, 1976, 'Peer Teaching in Higher Education: A Review', *Higher*

Education, 5, pp.9–33. An easy to read analysis of a variety of methods of peer teaching with a vast bank of references.

Good, H.M., 1978, 'Interview Marking of Examination Scripts', *Assessment in Higher Education*, 3(2), pp.122–37. An outline of a method of marking examination scripts with the student present, ensuring feedback and assisting learning.

Gosling, W., 1978, *Microprocessors, Society and Education* (C.E.T., London). A short exposition on the likely changes in the near future.

Hamilton, D. *et al.* (eds.), 1977, *Beyond the Numbers Game: A Reader in Educational Evaluation* (Macmillan, London). One point of view in educational evaluation is elaborated by a careful choice of papers.

Harris, N.D.C., 1975, 'What is Assessment?', *Assessment in Higher Education*, 1(1), pp.5–12. A brief outline of a variety of ways of viewing assessment: predictive, diagnostic, comparative, absolute, formative and summative.

Harris, N.D.C. and Kirkhope, S., 1977, *An Evaluation of the Use of Self Instructional Materials in the Library* (University of Bath, Educational Services Unit, Bath). Also in *CORE*, 2(1), fiche 1B4–2D7. An evaluation of the use of study packs and video-cartridges in a library including costs, student's reactions and suggestions for modification.

Harrow, A.J., 1972, *A Taxonomy of the Psychomotor Domain* (McKay, New York). An attempt to provide a hierarchy of learning levels in this domain.

Hartog, P. and Rhodes, E.C., 1935, *An Examination of Examinations* (Macmillan, London). Most of the criticisms of examinations raised are still applicable today.

Heim, A., 1976, *Teaching and Learning in Higher Education* (National Foundation for Educational Research, London). An easy to read book with a very personal approach by the author. Very useful for new lecturers, but with plenty of provocative ideas for the more experienced.

Hill, W.F., 1977, *Learning Thru Discussion* (Guide for Leaders and Members of Discussion Groups) (Sage Publications, Beverley Hills). A useful little booklet which outlines a clearly defined method for using discussion groups for learning purposes.

Hills, P.J., 1979, *Teaching and Learning as a Communication Process* (Croom Helm, London). Considers the teaching/learning process in terms of a communications model. Contains much practical advice for the teacher.

Hodgson, A.M., 1974, 'Structural Communication in Practice' in Howe, A. and Romiszowski, A.J. (eds.), *APLET Yearbook of Educational and Instructional Technology 1974/5* (Kogan Page, London). An elaboration of the use of and techniques for developing structural communication learning materials.

Hooper, R., 1977, *Computer Assisted Learning: Final Report of the Director* (Council for Educational Technology, London). Covers the programmes, achievements, effects, costs of computer-assisted learning and possibilities for the future.

Horn, R. and Green, J., 1974, 'Information Mapping' in Howe, A. and Romiszowski, A.J. (eds.), *APLET Yearbook of Educational and Instructional Technology 1974/5* (Kogan Page, London). An outline of the use of information mapping in education.

Howe, M.J.A. and Godfrey, J., 1977, *Student Note Taking as an Aid to Learning* (University of Exeter, Exeter University Teaching Services, Exeter). Evidence and guidelines based on several years of research by the principal author.

Hudson, L., 1966, *Contrary Imaginations* (Methuen, London). A small treatise on the different styles of thinking.

Katona, G., 1940, *Organizing and Memorizing* (Columbia University Press, New York). A report on a long series of experiments to demonstrate the difference between memorising and understanding.

Keller, F.S. and Sherman, J.G., 1974, *The Keller Plan Handbook* (W.A. Benjamin, London). A summary and guideline to the use of the proctorial style learning.

Klug, B., 1977, *The Grading Game* (National Union of Students, London). A very good short book which queries some of the present premisses of assessment and suggests some modifications, in particular profile marking. It is marred by the occasional political excursion.

Koestler, A., 1968, *The Sleepwalkers* (Hutchinson, London). The book illustrates that the great discoverers proceed by a mixture of unconscous assumption, intuition and self-contradiction. It is a comprehensive survey of man's changing ideas about the universe in which the author queries the apparent split between science and religion.

Krathwohl, D.R., Bloom, B.S., and Masia, B.B., 1964, *Taxonomy of Educational Objectives: Handbook 2, The Affective Domain* (Longmans, London). The companion book to Bloom's book on the cognitive domain. An attempt to deduce some order out of all the attitudes and motivation aspects of learning.

Landa, L.N., 1974, *Algorithmization in Learning and Instruction* (Educational Technology Publications, Englewood Cliffs). An account of the use of algorithms in the design of instruction and by students to aid their learning. Several case studies are included.

Leenders, M.R. and Erskine, J.A., 1973, *Case Research: The Case Writing Process* (Canada Research and Publication Division, The University of W. Ontario, London). An excellent book on the writing of and use of case studies.

Leggatt, R., 1970, *Showing Off* (National Committee on Audio Visual Aids in Education, London). A brief booklet giving lots of ideas on displays, simple non-projected visual aids, including layout, preparation, lettering, etc.

Macdonald-Ross, M., 1973, 'Behavioural Objectives: A Critical Review', *Instructional Science*, 2(1), pp.1–52. Not only an extended review giving the advantages and disadvantages of behavioural objectives, but also a short explanation of 'ends-means' versus 'means-ends' approach.

Mackenzie, N., Eraut, M. and Jones, H.C., 1970, *Teaching and Learning: An Introduction to New Methods and Resources in Education* (UNESCO and International Association of Universities, Paris). An outline of a systematic approach to higher education which still seems very up to date.

McLeish, J., 1968, *The Lecture Method* (Cambridge Institute of Education) (Monographs on Teaching Methods No. 1), Cambridge). A small classic on the lecture method which has not dated.

McLuhan, M., 1964, *Understanding Media* (Sphere Books Ltd., London). An unusual look at 'media' from his own definition of media. McLuhan attempts to elaborate the theme that the medium determines the message. Not an easy book to read.

Mager, R.F., 1957, *Preparing Instructional Objectives* (Fearon, Belmont, California). A little classic on behavioural objectives.

——, 1972, *Goal Analysis* (Fearon, Belmont, California). Do you have difficulty in setting out goals or purposes of the students learning? This little book should help you.

Mansell, A., 1976, 'Project Work in the Final Year of the Physics Course in the Department of Physics at Bristol University' in Group for Research and Innovation in Higher Education, 1976, *Studies in Laboratory Innovation* (The Nuffield Foundation, London). A report indicating the cost in terms of finance and technical assistance.

Markle, S., 1969, *Good Frames and Bad* (Wiley, New York). An eclectic programme on methods of developing programmed learning.

Marton, F., 1975, *On Non Verbatim Learning: I. Level of Processing and Level of Outcome* (Institute of Education, University of Goteborg, Publication No. 39, Goteborg). A discrimination between superficial and in-depth learning is outlined.

——, 1975, *On Non Verbatim Learning: II. The Erosion Effect of Task Induced Learning Algorithm* (Institute of Education, University of Goteborg, Publication No. 40, Goteborg). Outlines the use of mathemagenics, its advantageous and deleterious effects, based on experimental work.

Matthews, J., 1974, *The Use of Objective Tests* (School of Education, University of Lancaster (Teaching in Higher Education Series No. 9), Lancaster). The advantages and disadvantages of objective tests are covered. Guidance is given on the range of formats and the appropriate purposes for use of objective tests in relation to other methods of assessment and teaching.

Middendorf, W.H., 1971, 'Pacing Engineering Design Projects', *Engineering Education, 61*(6), pp.532–3. An example of the use of PERT (Programmed Evaluation and Review Technique).

Miller, C.M.L. and Parlett, M., 1974, *Up to the Mark: A Study of the Examination Game* (Society for Research into Higher education, Guildford). A study of examinations, their use, and students' reactions to a variety of methods at the University of Edinburgh.

Miller, G.A., 1970, *The Psychology of Communication* (Penguin, Harmondsworth). Seven essays covering: memory, processing information, human link in communication systems, psychical research, psycholinguistics, computers and communication, grammar.

Millerson, G., 1976, *Effective TV Production* (Focal Press, London). An excellent basic guide to TV production.

Morgan, A.S., 1976, 'Learning through Projects', *Studies in Higher Education, 1*(1), pp.63–8. An outline of the approach to the study of architecture through projects. He outlines some clear elements of project work.

Oppenheim, A.M., 1966, *Questionnaire Design and Attitude Measurement* (Heinemann, London). A well written basic text on questionnaire design which most lecturers will find full of useful ideas, hints and 'don'ts'.

Page, C.F., 1971, *Technical Aids to Teaching in Higher Education*

(Society for Research into Higher Education, Guildford). A short booklet giving a range of projected aids and some examples of their use in higher education.

——, 1974, *Student Evaluation of Teaching: The American Experience* (Society for Research into Higher Education, Guildford). A survey of some methods used in the USA, including the role of student evaluation in promotion of academic staff.

Parry, J., 1967, *The Psychology of Human Communiction* (University of London Press, London). The book offers answers to four questions: What are the chief types of information human beings transmit to one another? What are the barriers to transmission? What sort of communication issues characterise the more complex human activities? What are the trends in research and how far can they be pressed?

Pask, G., 1975, *Conversation, Cognition and Learning: A Cybernetic Theory and Methodology* (Elsevier, Amsterdam). A summary of the work of Pask and his colleagues up to 1975. A difficult book to read.

Popham, W.J. and Baker, E.L., 1970, *Systematic Instruction* (Prentice Hall, Englewood Cliffs). A short booklet outlining a systematic approach to instruction; rather naive in places.

Popper, K.R., 1974, *Conjectures and Refutations* (The Growth of Scientific Knowledge) (Routledge and Kegan Paul, London). A basic discourse on the philosophy of science in which the author suggests that there are no boundaries between science and metaphysics.

Postlethwaite, S.N., Novak, J.N. and Murray, H., 1971, *An Audio-Tutorial Approach to Learning* (Burgess Publishing Co., Minneapolis). An outline of the use of self-instructional materials in the form of audio recordings, displays, experiments, etc. associated with tutorial and assessment procedures.

Redfern, P.H., 1978, 'The Use of Research Papers in Examinations', *Assessment in Higher Education, 3*(2), p.159. A brief outline of a style of examination paper, requiring the analysis of data to determine conclusions, and the assumptions on which the conclusions are based.

Roach, K. and Hammond, R., 1976, 'Zoology by Self Instruction', *Studies in Higher Education, 1*(2), pp.179–96. An outline of the methods used by an institution to overcome the problems of rapid increases in student numbers on a course, which had to use the same resources of space and staff.

Rogers, C.R., 1969, *Freedom to Learn* (Merrill, New York). A plea for treating students as individuals.

Romiszowski, A.J., 1974, *The Selection and Use of Instructional Media* (Kogan Page, London). A systematic approach to the use of media based primarily on the behavioural approach.

Rothkopf, E.Z., 1972, 'Structural Text Features and the Control of Processes from Written Materials' in Carroll, J.B. and Freedle, R.D. (eds.), *Language Comprehension and the Acquisition of Knowledge* (Winston, Washington, D.C.). An outline of the use of questions within, before or after textual materials and their effect (see also Marton).

Rowntree, D., 1974, *Educational Technology in Curriculum Development* (Harper and Row, London). An excellent survey of the present state of the art in Educational Technology.

——, 1977, *Assessing Students: How Shall We Know Them?* (Harper and Row, London). A thought-provoking excursion into the fundamentals of assessment in all its aspects, written from the viewpoints of the assessor, the assessed and the recipients of assessment information.

Rushby, N.J., 1979, *An Introduction to Educational Computing* (Croom Helm, London).

Siegel, S., 1956, *Non-Parametric Statistics* (McGraw Hill, New York). A classic book on the use of statistics in areas of study where normal distributions and unequal number intervals apply (education?).

Simmons, D.D., 1974, *Notes on the Case Study* (The Case Clearing House of GB and Ireland, Cranfield). A series of notes covering the range from writing to the use of case studies, primarily in management studies.

Svennson, L., 1976, *Study Skill and Learning* (University of Goteborg Studies in Educational Sciences, Publication No. 19, Goteborg, Sweden). The in-depth results of a study into study skill and learning related to educational practice in schools and universities.

Wankowski, J.A., 1977, 'Learning How to Learn at University: The Case for an Experimental Centre', *British Journal of Guidance and Counselling, 5,* pp.41–8. A proposal for a centre where students and tutors can improve their tuition and study skills. The basis would be self-tuition.

Wertheimer, M., 1943, *Productive Thinking* (Harper Bros, New York). A basic case study approach to gestalt psychology.

Whitehead, A.N., 1932, *The Aims of Education* (Williams and

Horgte, London). Still a classic!

Wittich, W.A. and Schuller, C.F., 1973, *Instructional Technology: Its Nature and use* (Harper Bros, New York). A much revised but well established book on audio visual presentations and educational technology. Although many of the ideas are aimed at schools, it is a good source of ideas.

Wyant, T.G., 1974, 'Network Analysis' in Howe, A. and Romiszowski, A.J. (eds.), *APLET Yearbook of Educational and Instructional Technology 1974/5* (Kogan Page, London). An outline of the use of network analysis in education.

GLOSSARY

Active Learning A learning situation in which the student is required to take an active part, for example, use a set of guide lines and resources from which to meet the requirements.

Affective Learning Learning which involves the development of or a change in attitudes; the levels of involvement in learning varying from awareness to development of a life philosophy based on the ideas being learned. (See also *motivation*.)

Aim A very general statement of the purpose of an institution or course. The statement does not give enough detail to enable any assessment to be made, but it does give enough information to judge the worth of goals, purposes or objectives.

Algorithm A set of instructions which lead to a termination point within a decision chain, provided the questions or decision bases are within the repertoire of the user.

Alphanumeric Usually referring to a display system which limits information to the use of letters of the alphabet and numbers.

Analysis In educational terms this usually refers to a particular method of subdividing a problem in order to make decisions. Examples are: algorithms, network analysis, critical path analysis.

Assessment Any method of attempting to determine a learner's performance. Examples are: examinations, assignments, projects, dissertations, viva voce.

Assignment A piece of work which a student is required to carry out either to enable him to learn or to give evidence that he has studied. The work is usally carried out without formal supervision either in a fixed time or to be completed by a particular date.

Atomistic (Learner) A style of learning which develops ideas piece by piece; often the sequence of pieces can be repeated without a clear understanding of the whole. Some learners are very good at learning in this style. (See also *holist*.)

Audio Tape A magnetic coated tape which is used to record signals which have been produced from sounds within the range of frequencies that the human ear can detect. The same recorded signal can be detected and transferred back to a sound.

Audio-Tutorial A style of learning where materials are provided for the learner to work on his own. The main communication medium to explain and discuss is the audio tape. The audio tape is usually supplemented by displays, experiments, slides or any other suitable means. Students have weekly meetings with tutors in groups.

Audio Visual Aid A term used to include *teaching aids* which are dependent on the use of audio and/or visual (usually pictorial) communication channels. Examples are: TV, film, language laboratory.

Behavioural Approach An approach to learning in which the student's expected behaviour after learning is pre-specified. The specification usually includes (a) the expected performance, (b) the conditions under which the performance will be demonstrated, and (c) the level of performance.

Behavioural Objectives A type of objective associated with the behavioural approach to learning. The expected behaviour of the student after learning is pre-specified. (See also *objectives*, *behavioural approach*.

Bits of Information The amount of information needed to make a decision between two equally likely alternatives. For example, if we need to decide whether a building is more or less than 30 m high we need one bit of information, two bits will enable us to make a decision among four equally likely alternatives, four bits will give sixteen alternatives; i.e. 2x alternatives require x bits of information.

Buzz Groups A small group of students (say four) who are required to solve a small problem within a large group situation (e.g. a lecture). The group can be required to report on their findings.

Carrel An individual study space usually identified by some kind of barrier between a similar working space. The carrel may or may not have associated audio visual facilities (called 'wet' and 'dry' carrels respectively).

Case Study This is an educational method to give students the opportunity to become a decision-maker or a problem-solver in a particular context. The student gains analytical and planning skills in a simulated situation. (See also *simulation*, *role playing*.)

Cefax An alphanumeric display system for television receivers transmitted by normal channels of the British Broadcasting Corporation. A special receiver is needed.

Chalkboard Another name for a 'blackboard', which allows for variations in the colour of the surface.

Cognitive Learning Learning which is specifically related to knowledge; analysis of knowledge and the creative aspects of knowledge.

Computer-Assisted Learning Learning in which the computer is used as a means of simulating situations, industrial complexes, etc., and/or in which the learner interacts with the computer.

Computer-Managed Learning Learning in which the computer either tests the student and gives information on progress or gives possible learning routes based on information provided.

Concept A classification or network of knowledge which enables the learner to recognise and internalise his environment.

Constraints Any external conditions which prevent an educational experience operating in an ideal way. Examples are: arrangement of seating, environmental conditions, shortage of resources.

Continuing Education Education which continues after the normal school leaving age; often associated with education throughout life.

Converger A learner whose character or experience causes them to react by accepting ideas or concepts that are provided in books, lectures or by any other means.

Cost Effectiveness The outcome of a course measured in terms of the cost. For example, if a course was reduced in length by 10 per cent, saving staff time, student time, and resources, and the results in examinations and tests showed only a marginal deterioration, the reduction is cost effective.

Creativity A term used to describe a human ability which enables that person to devise original ideas, designs, developments or innovations.

Criterion References Testing (Measurement) A type of testing where each item (question) in the test is related to a particular objective, goal or purpose. The measure of a student's success is how many he gets right, not how much better or worse he does when compared with other students.

Critical Path Analysis Usually based on a display or chart showing the relationships between the parts of a system. The time for each part is given and the longest path (in time) is the critical path.

Curriculum A description of all the elements of the learning experience provided in an institution or in formal learning. Sometimes the word is only associated with cognitive aspects displayed in syllabuses.

Cybernetics A study of control systems where particular importance is given to feedback of information. The effects of feedback on the system are carefully measured and monitored for effect. Such systems have applications within education (see, for example, Pask, 1975).

De-Briefing A means of enabling a group of students who have been involved in an active learning situation to consider analytically what has taken place and what can be learned from the experience.

Demonstrator A graduate student who is used in a laboratory to help undergraduate students.

Didactic The form of learning in which there is a detailed explanation given by the lecturer to which the learners listen.

Disciplinary Approach Learning based on subject basis (e.g. mathematics, history). The approach aims to elaborate the methodology of the discipline and the existing structures and jargon.

Discovery Learning Learning in which the resources have been devised to enable the learner to find relationships, laws and hypotheses without actually being told.

Dissertation An extended essay in which the student is expected to research existing ideas and to develop some of his own either by experimental or theoretical means.

Diverger A learner whose character or experience causes them to react by rejecting ideas or concepts that are provided in books, lectures or by any other means.

Domain Referenced Testing (Measurement) A form of testing based on the assumption that learning is associated with clumps or domains of knowledge. The tests can be devised by sampling the domains using items (questions). From the performance on the sample, a prediction can be made on the overall performance of a learner.

Educational Technology A systematic approach to the application of research data and varieties of methods, modes and media to improve learning. Historically it is associated with the behavioural approach and programmed learning, but is no longer based exclusively on these approaches.

Electronic Blackboard A device which enables the recording of written text or drawings on an audio cassette together with the spoken commentary. The replay is through a special piece of equipment connected to a normal TV set.

Evaluation An attempt to measure the worth of something — in this context the worth of a course/lecture etc.

Examination Usually a series of questions or tests which the student must complete in a fixed time without assistance. An examination is usually attended by lecturers to ensure that no cheating or copying occurs.

Feedback In education this usually means giving learners and teachers the knowledge of results of any form of assessment quickly. In some cases the feedback may also incorporate confirmation or correction of the learner's response to the assessment, allowing the student to adjust or adapt his learning.

Feedback Classroom A special form of classroom in which each student has a means of responding to questions asked by the lecturer. The means of response can be a simple coloured card which is displayed, or a complex electrical system where the student has several switches and the lecturer has meters which display individual and/or group results.

Further Education Education beyond the compulsory leaving age (16) or education to which students transfer after completing their first public examinations at school (age 15 or 16).

Games (Gaming) In an educational sense used to describe games that are set up to simulate life (e.g. in industry, government, decision-making, etc.).

Gestalt Approach A type of psychology which advocates learners finding out ideas and concepts for themselves without being told by the lecturer. (See also *discovery learning*.)

Goals A general term covering expectations of attitude, appreciation or understanding from the learner. The goals are usually given in a form which describes the learner's expected development of or change of attitude, appreciation or understanding. (See also *aim*, *objective*, *purpose*.)

Graduate Assistants A term primarily used in the United States to describe graduates who assist in the education of undergraduates by taking on some tutorial roles.

Guided Discovery Learning in which the resources have been very carefully structured to ensure that a large proportion of learners discover the idea, principle, etc. (See also *discovery learning*.)

Haptic (Learner) A learner who, in a visual sense, analyses the visual presentation into elements (a visual version of *atomistic*).

Hardware In education this usually refers to equipment. Examples are: projectors, recorders, cameras, computers.

Heuristic Learning see *discovery learning*.

Higher Education Usually used to refer to that part of the educational system which is mainly concerned with learners studying for degrees.

Holist (Learner) A style of learning which sees ideas as a whole and not as a structure of pieces. Some learners are very good at learning in this style. (See also *atomistic*.)

Independent Learning A form of learning in which the learner has control over some or all of: purposes, content, means of learning, assessment.

Information Mapping A system which endeavours to identify, categorise and interrelate information that is required for learning and for reference.

Innovation In an educational sense the term 'innovation' is usually used to describe an unusual approach to providing learning situations.

Keller Plan A system of learning in which clear objectives, related resources, and mastery testing procedures are used. The tests are marked by senior students on the same course. The students are self-paced but are expected to master the unit before progressing.

Key Words A series of words which are used to enable a search for information. For example, 'tests' would give all references to tests; 'criterion-referenced' would give all references to the theory and practice of 'criterion-referencing'; 'criterion-referenced tests' would give those common to both.

Knowledge Facts, laws, principles, concepts or theories which form a framework or network.

Leaderless Group A group of learners who are required to carry out some activity for which no leader (lecturer) will be present.

Learner A person who is learning. (See also *atomistic, haptic, holist, serialist, sequential, syndicate of learners, visual learner, unequal learners.*)

Learning A person who is attempting to master or discover something of which he has limited previous experience or no previous experience. (See also *active learning, affective learning, cognitive learning, computer-assisted learning, computer-managed learning, discovery learning, heuristic learning, independent learning, mastery learning, passive learning, programmed learning, programmed learning, psychomotor learning, resource-based learning, rote learning, surface learning.*)

Linear Note A form of note taking dependent on headings and sub-headings.

Mass Media Those media used for mass communication. Examples are: television, newspapers, radio.

Mastery Learning A form of learning in which the learner has to demonstrate that he has mastered the topic by performing at a high level on the test provided.

Media The means by which a message is conveyed. Examples are:

print, film, magnetic tape.

Microfiche A photographic image on transparent sheet in which a large number of pages can be reproduced on a small area of photographic material, for example, 98 pages of A4 reduced to 147 mm x 103 mm.

Microteaching A technique usually used in the training of teachers. The teacher is required to perform small aspects of teaching (e.g. asking questions, demonstrating) to a small group of lerners. The performance is analysed (e.g. using a video recording) and the student is required to perform the task again in improved form with another small group of learners.

Modes A description given to the way in which learning takes place. Examples are: individual, small group, large group.

Motivation A term used to indicate the willingness of a learner to learn — if he is very willing he is said to be highly motivated. (See also *affective learning*.)

Network Analysis The name given to a particular style of presenting a chart of relationships. In an educational context it usually shows relationships between concepts in a course. (See also *critical path analysis*.)

Objectives The statement of the purpose of an activity, in particular the expected outcome of a piece of learning carried out by students. (See also *affective learning*, *behavioural objectives*, *cognitive learning*, *psychomotor learning*.)

Oracle An alphanumeric display system for television receivers transmitted by the normal channels of the Independent Broadcasting Authority. A special receiver is needed.

Passive Learning A learning situation in which the student is required to take a passive role, for example, watching instruction by television.

Patterned Note A form of note-taking in which the learner uses a central core with a network of labelled lines. The labelled lines are his perceived relationships between the parts of the notes (several examples are given in the text).

Peer Teaching Teaching by students at the same stage of learning or of the same age group.

Personalised System of Instruction (PSI) see *Keller plan*.

Pre-Requisites The expectations of a student's knowledge and ability before starting a new course.

Prestel A form of alphanumeric display and storage for use with television sets. The signal is received through a telephone cable to a receiver and interrogator. The system has, in theory, an infinite storage capacity (dependent on the associated computer system). There is no limit to the access. The user can also have material stored which he can make accessible to other users or keep confidential. The system is operated by the Post Office. (See also *Cefax, Oracle*.)

Programmed Evaluation and Review Technique (PERT) A proposed system is submitted along with a list of specifications, a series of steps in the design of the system are listed. For each step the time taken is estimated from optimistic to pessimistic including the expected and the standard deviation. A critical path is deduced as a basis of action (see for example Middendorf, 1971).

Programmed Learning Usually associated with learning materials which have some or all of the following characteristics: (a) an analysis of the expected performance on completion, (b) carefully stated behavioural objectives, (c) a specific criterion-referenced test for the material, (d) minimum acceptable test performance on completion of the learning, (e) information given to students on their performance at various times during the learning sequence, and (f) the material has been tried in a pilot trial on an equivalent group of learners.

Project In an educational context a project is usally conceived as having three parts: (a) systematic planning and preparation, (b) fulfilment of an investigation, and (c) submission of a report and/or artefact.

Psychomotor Learning Learning which is associated with skills of movement and co-ordination. Examples are: speaking, listening, manual dexterity.

Pulsing System A system used with audio tapes in which a signal of short duration (a pulse) is used to activate a mechanism which changes the picture being viewed or which stops the playback machine.

Resource-Based Learning Used as a vague term to describe situations where the learning is not organised in a formal didactic manner, for example, the use of work-sheets and study packs.

Retention When a learner is able to remember what he has learned, we say retention has occurred.

Rote Learning Learning in which the expectation is that the learner will be able to repeat exactly what he has seen or heard, for example remembering multiplication tables.

Self-Instruction Learning materials used by a student without the presence of a tutor or without assistance from a tutor. Usually associated with formalised learning materials which are structured. Examples are: programmed learning, synchronised tape and slide.

Senior Students Students who are on the same course, but are at a later stage in the course (for example third-year students on an undergraduate course in relation to first-year students).

Sequential (Learner) A style of learning which sees learning in a sequence of parts. Some learners are very good at learning in this style. (See also *atomistic, holist.*)

Serialist (Learner) see *sequential.*

Simulation A substitute system compared to a real one is often used in learning. The real system may be too dangerous, too complex. Examples are: a computer simulation of a chemical plant, a computer simulation of a business.

Structural Communication A form of learning in which the material is structured. The objectives are stated and an extended presentation is given into which the learner must investigate and respond on a test. The basis of his response is used to give him information about his learning.

Structured Sequence A piece of learning material in which the sequence of learning has been carefully designed into parts. The sequence is said to be structured.

Study Pack A folder including one or more papers on a topic. The study pack may be used in conjunction with a work-sheet.

Surface Learning The accumulation of knowledge, usually required for repetition when tested.

Synchronised (tape/slide) A system which can be used to change automatically the picture and keep it in step (synchronisation) with an audio recording. Such systems can be used with 35 mm slides, filmstrips, microfiche and 8 mm film.

Syndicate of Learners A group of learners who meet together to discuss common problems or work together. The group is usually self-selected and arranges its own schedule of working.

Systems Approach A process involving the specification of objectives, and the modification of the process in relation to information received from the testing instruments. Such an approach can be applied to learning and to the management of learning.

Teaching Aid Some artefact which aids the teaching of a subject; there is a hidden assumption that the main part of the teaching is done by the teacher who administers and controls the aid. Examples are: overhead projector, slide projector, tape recorder, study pack, book.

Teletext Any system which is used to provide an alphanumeric display system on to a television screen. Usually associated with an electronic generation of the characters.

Terminal (Computer) Usually a keyboard (rather like a typewriter) by which the user can communicate with the computer through programs and routines already stored in the computer system.

Test An assessment from which the marks are not included in the marks which lead to a qualification or classification. (This is the meaning used in this book.) It can also be synonymous with *assessment*.

Unequal Learners Learners who are at different stages on the same course.

Video-Cartridge A videotape which is stored on one reel inside a container. When the container is placed in the machine the videotape is automatically fed through to a second reel inside the machine.

Video-Cassette A videotape already threaded between two reels inside a container. The reels can be side by side or on the same axis. When the container is put into the machine a mechanism threads a loop of the tape around the record and/or playback heads.

Videophone A telephone system in which you can see the other caller as well as hear them. The picture is on a small television screen.

Videotape A type of magnetic tape on which signals are recorded from a camera or other source. The signals can be sensed and used to produce a television picture.

Visual (Learner) A learner who, in a visual sense, views the whole and does not analyse it into parts (a visual version of *holist*; see also *haptic*).

Whiteboard A form of 'vertical' surface on which writing is done using a coloured pen. The surface can also be used for projection purposes. (An 'opposite' to a blackboard!)

Work-sheet (Work card) Any sheet (or card) which gives instructions, directions, or guidance to the learner on material, equipment or experimental work. For example, the learner may be required to use the contents of a study pack in order to write an assignment.

INDEX